LEARN MODERN GREEK IN 100 DAYS

THE 100% NATURAL METHOD TO FINALLY GET RESULTS WITH MODERN GREEK!

BEGINNER

NATURA LINGUA

LEARN MODERN GREEK IN 100 DAYS

TABLE OF CONTENTS

Welcome   xiii
The NaturaLingua Method   xvii
Additional Resources   xxi

BEFORE BEGINNING
Debunking Myths About Learning Modern
Greek   3
Why learning Modern Greek?   6
The Polyglots' Secret   9

INSTRUCTIONS
1. Learning to Read Modern Greek   15
Modern Greek Pronunciation Guide for
English Beginners   17
How to Use This Manual   21
And what about grammar?   27
Additional Resources   31

MODERN GREEK IN 100 DAYS
Important Notes   37
Ημέρα νούμερο 1: Χαιρετισμοί   38
Day 1: Greetings   39
Ημέρα νούμερο 2: Κοινές Εκφράσεις   40
Day 2: Common Expressions   41
Ημέρα νούμερο 3: Λεξιλόγιο Παρουσίασης   42
Day 3: Introduction Vocabulary   43
Ημέρα νούμερο 4: Προσωπική πληροφορία   44
Day 4: Personal Information   45
Ημέρα νούμερο 5: Κοινά ρήματα I   46
Day 5: Common Verbs I   47
Ημέρα νούμερο 6: Ποτά   48
Day 6: Beverages   49
Important Reminder Before Starting Lesson 7   50
                                                            51

Ημέρα αριθ. 7: Περιγραφικά Επίθετα Ι 52
Day 7: Descriptive Adjectives I 53
Ημέρα νούμερο 8: Τοποθεσία και
κατευθύνσεις Ι 54
Day 8: Location and Directions I 55
Ημέρα νούμερο 9: Τοποθεσία και οδηγίες ΙΙ 56
Day 9: Location and Directions II 57
Ημέρα νούμερο 10: Ερωτήσεις 58
Day 10: Questions 59
Challenge No. 1 # 60

61

Ημέρα νούμερο 11: Ημέρες και ώρα 62
Day 11: Days and Time 63
Ημέρα νούμερο 12: Ημέρες της εβδομάδας 64
Day 12: Days of the Week 65
Ημέρα νούμερο 13: Οικογένεια Ι 66
Day 13: Family I 67
Ημέρα νούμερο 14: Οικογένεια ΙΙ 68
Day 14: Family II 69
Ημέρα αρ. 15: Αριθμοί από 1 έως 10 70
Day 15: Numbers from 1 to 10 71
Ημέρα αριθ. 16: Αριθμοί από 11 έως 20 72
Day 16: Numbers from 11 to 20 73
Ημέρα νούμερο 17: Ψώνια Ι 74
Day 17: Shopping I 75
Ημέρα νούμερο 18: Ψώνια ΙΙ 76
Day 18: Shopping II 77
Ημέρα νούμερο 19: Μεταφορά Ι 78
Day 19: Transport I 79
Ημέρα νούμερο 20: Μεταφορά ΙΙ 80
Day 20: Transport II 81
Challenge No. 2 # 82

83

Ημέρα νούμερο 21: Τοποθεσία και Μέρη Ι 84
Day 21: Location and Places I 85
Ημέρα νούμερο 22: Επίθετα ΙΙ 86
Day 22: Adjectives II 87
Ημέρα νούμερο 23: Επίθετα ΙΙΙ 88
Day 23: Adjectives III 89

Ημέρα νούμερο 24: Χρώματα   90
Day 24: Colors   91
Ημέρα νούμερο 25: Ηλεκτρονικά και
τεχνολογία I   92
Day 25: Electronics and Technology I   93
Ημέρα νούμερο 26: Μήνες και εποχές   94
Day 26: Months and Seasons   95
Ημέρα νούμερο 27: Περισσότεροι μήνες και
εποχές   96
Day 27: Beyond months and seasons   97
Ημέρα νούμερο 28: Συναισθήματα I   98
Day 28: Feelings I   99
Ημέρα νούμερο 29: Συναισθήματα II   100
Day 29: Feelings II   101
Ημέρα αριθ. 30: Μέρη του Σώματος I   102
Day 30: Body Parts I   103
Challenge No. 3 #   104
    105

Ημέρα νούμερο 31: Μέρη του Σώματος II   106
Day 31: Body Parts II   107
Ημέρα νούμερο 32: Χρόνος και ημερολόγιο   108
Day 32: Time and Calendar   109
Ημέρα νούμερο 33: Τροφή I   110
Day 33: Food I   111
Ημέρα νούμερο 34: Τρόφιμα II   112
Day 34: Foods II   113
Ημέρα νούμερο 35: Ποτά και επιδόρπια   114
Day 35: Drinks and Desserts   115
Ημέρα νούμερο 36: Μαγειρική και κουζίνα   116
Day 36: Cooking and Kitchen   117
Ημέρα νούμερο 37: Ταξίδια και Τόποι II   118
Day 37: Travel and Places II   119
Ημέρα νούμερο 38: Επείγοντα και υγεία   120
Day 38: Emergencies and Health   121
Ημέρα νούμερο 39: Αριθμοί 21-30   122
Day 39: Numbers 21-30   123
Ημέρα νούμερο 40: Ημέρες της εβδομάδας   124
Day 40: Days of the Week   125
Challenge No. 4 #   126
    127

Ημέρα νούμερο 41: Καθαριότητα I 128

Day 41: Cleaning I 129

Ημέρα νούμερο 42: Καθαριότητα II 130

Day 42: Cleaning II 131

Ημέρα νούμερο 43: Κατεύθυνση και
τοποθεσία II 132

Day 43: Direction and Location II 133

Ημέρα νούμερο 44: Ψώνια III 134

Day 44: Shopping III 135

Ημέρα νούμερο 45: Χρήματα και πληρωμές 136

Day 45: Money and Payments 137

Ημέρα νούμερο 46: Καιρός και φύση 138

Day 46: Weather and Nature 139

Ημέρα νούμερο 47: Καταστροφές και
γεωγραφία 140

Day 47: Disasters and Geography 141

Ημέρα νούμερο 48: Χρώματα 142

Day 48: Colors 143

Ημέρα νούμερο 49: Τεχνολογία I 144

Day 49: Technology I 145

Ημέρα νούμερο 50: Τεχνολογία II 146

Day 50: Technology II 147

Challenge No. 5 # 148

149

Ημέρα νούμερο 51: Ζώα 150

Day 51: Animals 151

Ημέρα νούμερο 52: Φυτά και φύση 152

Day 52: Plants and Nature 153

Ημέρα νούμερο 53: Αριθμοί 31-40 154

Day 53: Numbers 31-40 155

Ημέρα νούμερο 54: Μουσική και διασκέδαση 156

Day 54: Music and Entertainment 157

Ημέρα νούμερο 55: Ταξίδι και Μεταφορά III 158

Day 55: Travel and Transportation III 159

Ημέρα νούμερο 56: Ψώνια II 160

Day 56: Shopping II 161

Ημέρα νούμερο 57: Σώμα και υγεία II 162

Day 57: Body and Health II 163

Ημέρα αριθ. 58: Επαγγέλματα και εργασία I 164

Day 58: Professions and Work I 165

Ημέρα νούμερο 59: Είδη οικιακής χρήσης II   166
Day 59: Household Items II   167
Ημέρα νούμερο 60: Μέτρα και μέγεθος   168
Day 60: Measurements and Size   169
Challenge No. 6 #   170
   171
Ημέρα αριθ. 61: Τροφή και Διατροφή II   172
Day 61: Food and Nutrition II   173
Ημέρα νούμερο 62: Ημέρες της εβδομάδας   174
Day 62: Days of the Week   175
Ημέρα αριθ. 63: Καιρός και εποχές   176
Day 63: Weather and Seasons   177
Ημέρα νούμερο 64: Οικογένεια II   178
Day 64: Family II   179
Ημέρα νούμερο 65: Κατευθύνσεις και
τοποθεσίες III   180
Day 65: Directions and Locations III   181
Ημέρα νούμερο 66: Συναισθήματα II   182
Day 66: Emotions II   183
Ημέρα νούμερο 67: Τεχνολογία και μέσα
ενημέρωσης   184
Day 67: Technology and Media   185
Ημέρα νούμερο 68: Ανάγνωση και τέχνες   186
Day 68: Reading and Arts   187
Ημέρα νούμερο 69: Ταξίδια και Τόποι II   188
Day 69: Travel and Places II   189
Ημέρα αριθμός 70: Αριθμοί 11-20   190
Day 70: Numbers 11-20   191
Challenge No. 7 #   192
   193
Ημέρα αριθ. 71: Αριθμοί από 21 έως 30   194
Day 71: Numbers from 21 to 30   195
Ημέρα νούμερο 72: Διάφορα I   196
Day 72: Miscellaneous I   197
Ημέρα νούμερο 73: Μαγειρική και κουζίνα II   198
Day 73: Cooking and Kitchen II   199
Ημέρα αριθ. 74: Ιατρικό και Υγεία II   200
Day 74: Medical and Health II   201
Ημέρα νούμερο 75: Εκπαίδευση και μάθηση   202
Day 75: Education and Learning   203

Ημέρα νούμερο 76: Χρήματα και Ψώνια ΙΙ   204

Day 76: Money and Shopping II   205

Ημέρα νούμερο 77: Φαγητό έξω ΙΙ   206

Day 77: Eating Out II   207

Ημέρα νούμερο 78: Σπίτι και έπιπλο ΙΙ   208

Day 78: House and Furniture II   209

Ημέρα νούμερο 79: Καιρός ΙΙ   210

Day 79: Weather II   211

Ημέρα νούμερο 80: Αναψυχή και χόμπι ΙΙ   212

Day 80: Leisure and Hobbies II   213

Challenge No. 8 #   214

    215

Ημέρα νούμερο 81: Μεταφορά ΙΙ   216

Day 81: Transport II   217

Ημέρα νούμερο 82: Φύση και Γεωγραφία ΙΙ   218

Day 82: Nature and Geography II   219

Ημέρα νούμερο 83: Χρόνος και ρουτίνα   220

Day 83: Time and Routine   221

Ημέρα νούμερο 84: Συναισθήματα ΙΙΙ   222

Day 84: Emotions III   223

Ημέρα νούμερο 85: Χρώματα και σχήματα   224

Day 85: Colors and Shapes   225

Ημέρα νούμερο 86: Σχέσεις   226

Day 86: Relationships   227

Ημέρα νούμερο 87: Ρούχα και αξεσουάρ   228

Day 87: Clothes and Accessories   229

Ημέρα νούμερο 88: Τεχνολογία και Μέσα Ενημέρωσης ΙΙ   230

Day 88: Technology and Media II   231

Ημέρα νούμερο 89: Τροφή και ποτά ΙΙ   232

Day 89: Food and Drinks II   233

Ημέρα νούμερο 90: Σπίτι και ζωή   234

Day 90: Home and Life   235

Challenge No. 9 #   236

    237

Ημέρα 91: Ψώνια και καταστήματα   238

Day 91: Shopping and Stores   239

Ημέρα νούμερο 92: Επείγον και ασφάλεια   240

Day 92: Emergency and Safety   241

Ημέρα αριθ. 93: Ταξίδια και Τόποι III   242
Day 93: Travel and Places III   243
Ημέρα αριθ. 94: Ζώα και κατοικίδια ζώα   244
Day 94: Animals and Pets   245
Ημέρα αριθ. 95: Εργασία και επάγγελμα   246
Day 95: Work and Profession   247
Ημέρα αριθ. 96: Ημέρες και μήνες   248
Day 96: Days and Months   249
Ημέρα αριθ. 97: Σώμα και υγεία   250
Day 97: Body and Health   251
Ημέρα νούμερο 98: Εκπαίδευση και
Μάθηση II   252
Day 98: Education and Learning II   253
Ημέρα νούμερο 99: Διάφορα II   254
Day 99: Miscellaneous II   255
Ημέρα νούμερο 100: Συγχαρητήρια για τον
ολοκλήρωση του εγχειριδίου   256
Day 100: Congratulations on completing the
manual   257
Challenge No. 10 #   258
   259

CONGRATULATIONS AND NEXT STEPS
Congratulations   263
What's Next?   265
Additional Resources   267
About the Author   269
Share Your Experience   270
By the Same Author   271

Essential Glossary   273

WELCOME

Imagine: you're walking around in Athens, understanding and speaking Greek naturally. Phrases spontaneously emerge in your mind, and you navigate this new language with ease and fluidity.

That's the goal of this manual.

If you're reading these lines, it's because you wish to master Greek. Whether for work or pleasure, the goal remains the same: to achieve it. The problem lies in the lack of time. Good courses to learn Greek in English are rare, and often, the available methods are complicated or ineffective.

But your motivation is intact! That's why you've tried apps promising wonders in just a few minutes a day. The result? More time spent collecting badges than acquiring real skills in Greek. You've tried traditional textbooks, often too complex and focused on grammar. Perhaps you've even considered classical courses, incompatible with your schedule.

My name is François, and I'm French. I am well acquainted with this situation.

A few years ago, I went to do a year of volunteering in Ukraine. To be effective, I had to quickly learn Ukrainian, Russian and English. But most learning resources were either too superficial or too complex.

Even worse, despite my motivation and long hours in front of my screen or immersed in manuals, the results were not forthcoming. I felt frustrated, angry, wondering why language learning seemed so easy for some and so difficult for me.

I was about to give up, thinking I was not cut out for languages.

Then, one evening, I met an English polyglot who spoke 11 languages. Impressed by his linguistic abilities, I asked him for his secret. His answer, as simple as it was unexpected, was that one should not study a language, but live it! One must learn a new language as one learned their mother tongue.

Intrigued, I followed his advice.

After all, I hadn't learned my mother tongue through conjugation tables or collecting badges. No, I learned French by imitating those around me, by communicating with my friends and family.

So, I abandoned my textbooks and removed the conjugation tables from the walls of my room.

I started listening to podcasts in English, watching movies in Ukrainian and Russian, and engaging in my first conversations. Forgetting grammar and conjugation, I simply used these languages. The results were quick to come: I increasingly understood daily conversations, with words and phrases naturally coming to mind.

My English friend was right: it worked.

Just as it's more effective to learn to swim by jumping into the water rather than reading a book on swimming, learning a foreign language is done by immersing oneself in the language, practicing conversation, listening, and adapting to the culture and linguistic nuances, rather than limiting oneself to the theoretical study of grammar rules and vocabulary.

This is the approach I propose in this Natura Lingua manual.

From the first lesson, you will fully immerse yourself in Greek.

In a few days, or even weeks, you will start to build a lexical foundation and mental mechanisms that will allow you to understand and communicate naturally in most daily situations.

Be aware, Natura Lingua is not a miracle solution. To get results, you will need to follow one lesson a day for 100 days.

But if you're ready to make this effort, then anyone can succeed with our method, based directly on the mechanisms that allowed you to learn your mother tongue.

If you've already learned your mother tongue, why couldn't you learn Greek?

Καλή τύχη,

François

THE NATURALINGUA METHOD

Natura Lingua offers you a natural and intuitive approach that transforms the language learning experience. Every educational content is meticulously optimized to enable you to acquire a new language up to 10 times faster and more efficiently than traditional methods.

Each Natura Lingua manual is based on four innovative principles that reinvent the way languages are learned.

1. The Funnel Principle

We've rigorously analyzed and filtered hundreds of thousands of words to retain only those that are essential in daily conversations. Thanks to this principle, you quickly develop a high level of understanding without wasting your time on superfluous terms.

2. Contextual Assimilation

Each term is introduced in a natural setting, reflecting common daily interactions. The result? A smooth assimilation of hundreds of terms and expressions, without ever feeling like you're actually studying.

3. Progressive Overload

Each lesson meticulously presents new words while reintroducing those already studied. Thus, day by day, you continuously progress while consolidating what you've learned.

4. Multiple Integrated Revisions

Gone are the days when vocabulary seemed to evaporate from your memory. Our unique method ensures that each term is reintroduced at strategic intervals in subsequent lessons. You revisit each term up to four times, reinforcing its memorization without even realizing it.

The Mechanism

What makes "Natura Lingua" so effective is its natural and gradual learning. Each lesson introduces new words in bold while reusing words from previous lessons. Additionally, each lesson is enriched with a "Grammatical Note" to illuminate key aspects of the language and a "Cultural Note" to avoid faux pas during conversations with natives.

Is It For Me?

If you're looking to speak a new language without getting lost in the intricacies of grammar, this manual is for you. However, if you love complex grammatical rules and endless vocabulary lists, then this manual is not for you.

Integrating the Manual Into Your Daily Life

Create a routine: dedicate a slot each day for your 15-minute lesson. A coffee in hand, your manual open in front of you, and off you go!

NB. I highly recommend downloading the audio that accompanies the lessons. It will greatly enhance your understanding and pronunciation. Using this manual without the audio is like enjoying toast without jam: you're missing the essence.

ADDITIONAL RESOURCES

DOWNLOAD THE RESOURCES ASSOCIATED WITH THIS MANUAL AND GREATLY ENHANCE YOUR CHANCES OF SUCCESS.

Scan this QR code to access them:

SCAN ME

👉 **https://www.natura-lingua.com/download**

• **Optimize your learning with audio:** To significantly improve your language skills, we strongly advise you to download the audio files accompanying this manual. This will enhance your listening comprehension and pronunciation.

• **Enhance your learning with flashcards:** Flashcards are excellent tools for vocabulary memorization. We highly encourage you to use them to maximize your results. Download our set of cards, specially designed for this manual.

• **Join our learning community:** If you're looking to connect with other language enthusiasts through "Natura Lingua", we invite you to join our online group. In this community, you'll have the opportunity to ask questions, find learning partners, and share your progress.

• **Explore more with other Natura Lingua manuals:** If you like this method, note that there are other similar manuals for different languages. Discover our complete collection of manuals to enrich your linguistic learning experience in a natural and progressive way.

We are here to support you in learning the target language. For optimal results, we highly recommend downloading the audio and using the flashcards. These additional resources are designed to further facilitate your journey.

Happy learning!

BEFORE BEGINNING

DEBUNKING MYTHS ABOUT
LEARNING MODERN GREEK

When it comes to learning new languages, Modern Greek often gets wrapped in myths that can deter potential learners before they even begin. One popular but incorrect belief is that Greek is an "exotic" language, too different from English or other Indo-European languages to learn effectively. This misconception, among others, not only misrepresents the language but also discourages enthusiastic learners. Let's debunk these myths and shed light on the true nature of learning Modern Greek.

Myth 1: Greek is Too Difficult for English Speakers

One of the most common myths is that Greek is exceptionally hard for English speakers due to its unique alphabet and grammatical structure. While it's true that Greek uses a different alphabet and has its own linguistic rules, this doesn't make it impossibly difficult. Many English words have Greek roots, especially in fields like science, medicine, and philosophy, providing a familiar foundation. Moreover, the Greek alphabet can be learned relatively quickly, serving as a stepping stone rather than a barrier.

Myth 2: You Need to Be Fluent to Communicate

Another misconception is that you need to achieve fluency before you can effectively communicate in Greek. However, the reality is that even basic knowledge can go a long way. Greeks are known for their hospitality and appreciate any effort made to speak their language. Simple phrases and greetings can open doors, and many Greeks are eager to help you learn.

Myth 3: There Are Not Enough Resources Available

Some believe that resources for learning Modern Greek are scarce compared to more widely spoken languages. While Greek may not have the same volume of materials as Spanish or French, there is a wealth of resources available online, including apps, websites, and interactive courses. The key is knowing where to look and being resourceful in your learning approach.

Myth 4: It's Only Useful in Greece

Thinking that Greek is only useful within Greece is a narrow perspective. Greek is not only spoken in Greece and Cyprus but also in diaspora communities around the world. Learning Greek can enhance travel experiences, unlock access to ancient texts in their original language, and connect you with a vibrant global community. Moreover, learning any new language improves cognitive skills and cultural understanding.

Myth 5: It's Too Late to Start

Finally, the myth that there's an age limit to learning languages is entirely unfounded. Success stories abound of people who began learning Greek later in life, whether for travel, heritage, or intellectual curiosity. The key to success is consistent practice, not age.

The real challenge of learning Modern Greek isn't wrapped up in its alphabet or availability of resources; it's about overcoming the initial intimidation and committing to the journey. Language learning is a marathon, not a sprint, and Greek is no exception. The rewards of being able to communicate, understand a rich cultural heritage, and access a new worldview far outweigh the initial hurdles.

In conclusion, the myths surrounding the learning of Modern Greek do a disservice to a language that is not only beautiful and rich in history but also accessible with the right mindset and approach. By debunking these myths, we can open the door to more people discovering the joy and benefits of learning Greek. The real challenge lies not in the language itself but in the perseverance and dedication of the learner. With commitment, anyone can embark on the rewarding journey of learning Modern Greek.

WHY LEARNING MODERN GREEK?

If you're reading this text, it's because you're interested in learning Modern Greek.

Let's talk about motivation. Learning a new language is a journey filled with challenges and rewards, and finding the right motivation can turn the process into an exciting adventure. Here are seven sources of inspiration to stimulate your desire to learn Modern Greek:

1. **Connect with History and Culture:** Modern Greek is a gateway to one of the world's richest histories and cultures. Imagine reading the works of Homer, Plato, and Aristotle in their original language or understanding the stories behind the ancient ruins and Byzantine churches. Learning Greek connects you directly to the roots of Western civilization.

. . .

2. **Enhance Your Travel Experiences:** Greece is a country of breathtaking landscapes, from the Aegean islands to the mountainous mainland. Speaking Greek will transform your travel experiences, allowing you to interact with locals, understand the culture deeply, and navigate the country with ease.

3. **Boost Your Career Opportunities:** Greece's strategic location at the crossroads of Europe, Asia, and Africa makes it a significant player in international trade, tourism, and shipping. Proficiency in Greek can open doors to career opportunities in various sectors, including diplomacy, archaeology, and the maritime industry.

4. **Unlock a Rich Literary and Philosophical Tradition:** Modern Greek literature is vibrant and diverse, with Nobel laureates like Odysseas Elytis and Giorgos Seferis. Delving into Greek philosophy, you'll engage with the thoughts that have shaped Western intellectual history, gaining insights into democracy, ethics, and metaphysics.

5. **Experience the Warmth of Greek Hospitality:** Greeks are renowned for their hospitality. Speaking their language allows you to experience this warmth and friendliness more authentically, making lifelong friends and perhaps even becoming part of a Greek family.

. . .

6. **Challenge Your Brain:** Learning a new language is an excellent way to keep your brain active and healthy. Greek, with its unique alphabet and structure, provides a stimulating challenge that can improve memory, cognitive skills, and even ward off brain aging.

7. **Enjoy Greek Cuisine:** Greek cuisine is a feast for the senses, and knowing the language will enrich your culinary experiences. You'll be able to order with confidence in tavernas, understand the ingredients and recipes, and maybe even cook authentic Greek dishes yourself.

Learning Modern Greek is not just about mastering a language; it's about opening yourself to a world of new experiences, ideas, and connections. It's a journey that can enrich your life in countless ways. So, let this be your call to action: embrace the challenge, persevere in your studies, and don't give up. The rewards of speaking Greek are vast and varied, waiting for you to explore. Keep pushing forward, and let your love for the language and its culture be your guide. Καλή τύχη! (Good luck!)

THE POLYGLOTS' SECRET

Have you ever thought that learning multiple languages was only for geniuses? Take Cardinal Giuseppe Mezzofanti, for example—he's said to have spoken between 38 and 72 languages, depending on the source. And what makes it even more impressive is that he did it in a time without the internet, apps, or all the resources we have today. Another amazing example is Kato Lomb, a Hungarian interpreter who spoke 16 languages fluently and could handle 11 more.

But how did they do it?

These language masters understood something many people miss. Learning a language doesn't have to mean complicated textbooks, intense courses, or years of effort. Mezzofanti and Lomb used a simpler, more natural approach. For them, learning wasn't a chore or an impossible task—it was a smooth, almost instinctive process.

. . .

What if learning a language wasn't as hard as you think?

A lot of people believe that becoming a polyglot takes a special gift or years of hard work. But that's not true. Learning a language is often much easier than it seems. What feels like a huge challenge is really just about using the right method.

Mezzofanti learned by translating religious texts, while Kato Lomb translated foreign books she found in libraries. This helped them learn quickly and naturally. Their secret? Consistency and immersion through translation. By translating texts from a foreign language into their own, and then back again, they slowly mastered the language.

So how can you do the same?

You don't need expensive courses or complicated techniques. Start with simple texts in the language you want to learn, translate them into your own language, and then back again. This simple method helps you absorb the language and its structure naturally.

Now's the time to get started.

With the NaturaLingua method, inspired by the natural approaches of Mezzofanti and Lomb, you can finally break through the language barrier. Don't let fear or misconceptions stop you. Jump in and enjoy the process of learning, understanding, and speaking a new language, one translation at a time. Are you ready to take on the challenge and add new languages to your life?

INSTRUCTIONS

LEARNING TO READ MODERN GREEK

Modern Greek Alphabet

1. **A, α (Alpha)** - Sounds like 'a' in "father".

2. **B, β (Beta)** - Sounds like 'v' in "vase".

3. **Γ, γ (Gamma)** - Sounds like 'g' in "go" (before 'a', 'o', 'u') or 'y' in "yes" (before 'e', 'i').

4. **Δ, δ (Delta)** - Sounds like 'th' in "this".

5. **E, ε (Epsilon)** - Sounds like 'e' in "met".

6. **Z, ζ (Zeta)** - Sounds like 'z' in "zebra".

7. **H, η (Eta)** - Sounds like 'ee' in "see".

8. **Θ, θ (Theta)** - Sounds like 'th' in "think".

9. **I, ι (Iota)** - Sounds like 'ee' in "see".

10. **K, κ (Kappa)** - Sounds like 'k' in "kite".

11. **Λ, λ (Lambda)** - Sounds like 'l' in "lion".

12. **M, μ (Mu)** - Sounds like 'm' in "mother".

13. **N, ν (Nu)** - Sounds like 'n' in "nose".

14. **Ξ, ξ (Xi)** - Sounds like 'x' in "fox".

15. **O, o (Omicron)** - Sounds like 'o' in "pot".

16. **Π, π (Pi)** - Sounds like 'p' in "pot".

17. **P, ρ (Rho)** - Rolled 'r', similar to Spanish "pero".

18. **Σ, σ/ς (Sigma)** - Sounds like 's' in "sun". Note: 'ς' is used at the end of a word.

19. **Τ, τ (Tau)** - Sounds like 't' in "top".

20. **Υ, υ (Upsilon)** - Sounds like 'f' in "few" or sometimes 'ee' in "see" depending on the word.

21. **Φ, φ (Phi)** - Sounds like 'f' in "file".

22. **Χ, χ (Chi)** - Similar to 'h' in "Bach" or Scottish "loch".

23. **Ψ, ψ (Psi)** - Sounds like 'ps' in "lapse".

24. **Ω, ω (Omega)** - Sounds like 'o' in "store".

This alphabet forms the foundation of Modern Greek pronunciation and is a critical step in learning how to read and speak the language effectively. With these sounds, you can begin to recognize and pronounce Greek words more accurately.

MODERN GREEK
PRONUNCIATION GUIDE FOR
ENGLISH BEGINNERS

Welcome to your quick guide to pronouncing Modern Greek! This guide will help you get started with the basics. Remember, practice makes perfect, so keep trying and listen to native speakers whenever possible.

Vowels

- **A, α (alpha)**: Pronounced like the "a" in "father". Example: Αθήνα (Athína) sounds like "ah-thee-nah".
- **E, ε (epsilon)**: Pronounced like the "e" in "bet". Example: Έλληνας (Éllinas) sounds like "eh-lee-nas".
- **H, η (eta), I, ι (iota), Y, υ (upsilon), EI, ει, OI, οι, YI, υι**: All pronounced like the "ee" in "see". Examples: Ηλίας (Ilías) sounds like "ee-lee-as", Οικονομία (Oikonomía) sounds like "ee-ko-no-mee-ah".

17

- **O, o (omicron)**: Pronounced like the "o" in "pot". Example: Όχι (Óchi) sounds like "o-hee".
- **Ω, ω (omega)**: Pronounced like the "o" in "store". Example: Ωραίος (Oraíos) sounds like "o-ray-os".
- **ΑΥ, αυ (before a voiced sound)**: Sounds like "av" in "average". Example: Αυγό (Avgó) sounds like "av-go".
- **ΑΥ, αυ (before a voiceless sound)**: Sounds like "af" in "aftershock". Example: Αυτό (Aftó) sounds like "af-to".
- **ΕΥ, ευ (before a voiced sound)**: Sounds like "ev" in "event". Example: Ευχαριστώ (Efcharistó) sounds like "ef-ha-ree-sto".
- **ΕΥ, ευ (before a voiceless sound)**: Sounds like "ef" in "effect". Example: Ευτυχία (Eftychía) sounds like "ef-tee-hee-ah".

Consonants

- **Β, β (beta)**: Pronounced like the "v" in "vase". Example: Βίος (Víos) sounds like "vee-os".
- **Γ, γ (gamma)**: Before "ε", "η", "ι", "υ", sounds like the "y" in "yes". Example: Γη (Yi) sounds like "yee". Before "α", "o", "ω", it sounds like a soft "g" (but there's no exact English equivalent, think of the Spanish "g" in "agua").
- **Δ, δ (delta)**: Pronounced like the "th" in "this". Example: Δάσος (Dásos) sounds like "thah-sos".

- **Z, ζ (zeta)**: Pronounced like the "z" in "zebra".
  Example: Ζωή (Zoí) sounds like "zoh-ee".
- **Θ, θ (theta)**: Pronounced like the "th" in "think".
  Example: Θάλασσα (Thálassa) sounds like "thah-lah-ssa".
- **Κ, κ (kappa)**: Pronounced like the "k" in "kite".
  Example: Καλός (Kalós) sounds like "kah-los".
- **Λ, λ (lambda)**: Pronounced like the "l" in "lip".
  Example: Λόγος (Lógos) sounds like "loh-gos".
- **Μ, μ (mu)**: Pronounced like the "m" in "man".
  Example: Μήλο (Mílo) sounds like "mee-lo".
- **Ν, ν (nu)**: Pronounced like the "n" in "no". Example:
  Ναός (Naós) sounds like "nah-os".
- **Ξ, ξ (xi)**: Pronounced like the "x" in "box". Example:
  Ξένος (Xénos) sounds like "kseh-nos".
- **Π, π (pi)**: Pronounced like the "p" in "pot". Example:
  Πόδι (Pódi) sounds like "poh-dee".
- **Ρ, ρ (rho)**: Pronounced with a rolled "r". Example:
  Ρόδο (Ródo) sounds like "roh-doh".
- **Σ, σ/ς (sigma)**: Pronounced like the "s" in "sun".
  Example: Σπίτι (Spíti) sounds like "spee-tee".
- **Τ, τ (tau)**: Pronounced like the "t" in "top". Example:
  Τραγούδι (Tragoúdi) sounds like "tra-goo-dee".
- **Φ, φ (phi)**: Pronounced like the "f" in "fun".
  Example: Φως (Fos) sounds like "fos".
- **Χ, χ (chi)**: Pronounced like the "ch" in "loch" or the
  "j" in "jalapeño". Example: Χάρτης (Chártis) sounds
  like "har-tees".
- **Ψ, ψ (psi)**: Pronounced like "ps" in "lapse". Example:
  Ψάρι (Psári) sounds like "psah-ree".

Diphthongs

- **OY, ou**: Pronounced like the "oo" in "food".
  Example: Ουρανός (Ouranós) sounds like "oo-ra-nos".

Stress

In Greek, the stress of a word can change its meaning, so it's important to listen and repeat. The accent mark (΄) will tell you which syllable to stress.

This guide is a starting point. Listening to native speakers and practicing speaking will greatly improve your pronunciation. Enjoy your journey into the Greek language!

HOW TO USE THIS MANUAL

Phase No. 1:

1. Read the text in the language you are learning out loud, while listening to the corresponding audio (to be downloaded).
2. Try to translate the text into English, without consulting the translation.
3. Check with the official translation to complete yours.

This phase facilitates the assimilation of the language structure and vocabulary and reinforces understanding.

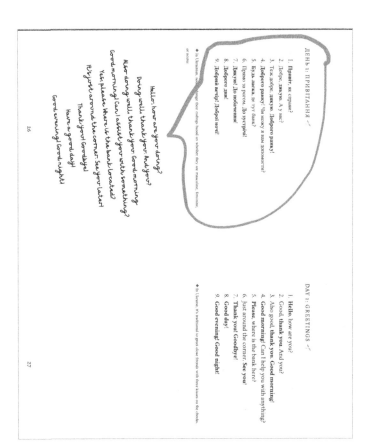

1. Привіт, як справи?
2. Добре, дякую. А у вас?
3. Теж добре, дякую. Доброго ранку!
4. Доброго ранку! Чи можу я вам допомогти?
5. Будь ласка, де тут банк?
6. Прямо за рогом. До зустрічі!
7. Дякую. До побачення!
8. Доброго дня!
9. Добрий вечір! Доброї ночі!

✦ In Ukrainian, ... change their endings based on whether they are masculine, feminine, or neuter.

Hello, how are you doing?
Doing well, thank you. And you?
Also doing well, thank you. Good morning.
Good morning! Can I assist you with something?
Yes please. Where is the bank located?
It's just around the corner. See you later.
Thank you! Goodbye!
Have a good day!
Good evening! Good night!

or notes

DAY 1: GREETINGS ✔

1. **Hello**, how are you?
2. Good, **thank you**. And you?
3. Also good, **thank you**. **Good morning!**
4. **Good morning!** Can I help you with anything?
5. **Please**, where is the bank here?
6. Just around the corner. **See you!**
7. **Thank you! Goodbye!**
8. **Good day!**
9. **Good evening! Good night!**

✦ In Ukraine, it's traditional to greet with close friends with three kisses on the cheeks.

Phase No. 1

Phase No. 2 (starting from lesson No. 7):

1. For each lesson starting from No. 7, first translate the text of that lesson (No. 7, No. 8, etc.) from the target language into English.
2. Then, go back 6 lessons and translate the English version of that lesson's text from English back into the target language, without referring to the original text.
3. Compare your translation with the original text of that lesson and adjust if necessary.
4. Read aloud the original text of that lesson, while listening to the audio.

This phase stimulates the activation of already acquired vocabulary and promotes the improvement of your communication skills.

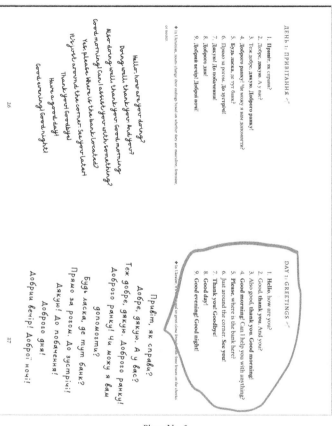

1. **Hello, how are you?**
2. Good, **thank you.** And you?
3. Also good, thank you. **Good morning!**
4. **Good morning!** Can I help you with anything?
5. **Please**, where is the bank here?
6. Just around the corner. **See you!**
7. **Thank you! Goodbye!**
8. **Good day!**
9. **Good evening! Good night!**

✦ In Ukraine... used to greet close friends. The three kisses on the cheeks

Привіт, як справи?
Добре, дякую. А у вас?
Теж добре, дякую. Доброго ранку!
Доброго ранку! Чи можу я вам
допомогти?
Будь ласка, де тут банк?
Прямо за рогом. До зустрічі!
Дякую! До побачення!
Доброго дня!
Добрий вечір! Доброї ночі!

ДЕНЬ 1: ПРИВІТАННЯ

1. **Привіт**, як справи?
2. Добре, дякую. А у вас?
3. Теж добре, дякую. **Доброго ранку!**
4. **Доброго ранку!** Чи можу я вам допомогти?
5. **Будь ласка**, де тут банк?
6. Прямо за рогом. **До зустрічі!**
7. **Дякую! До побачення!**
8. **Доброго дня!**
9. **Добрий вечір! Добраї ночі!**

✦ In Ukrainian, nouns change their endings based on whether they are masculine, feminine, or neuter.

Hello, how are you doing?
Doing well, thank you. And you?
Also doing well, thank you. Good morning!
Good morning! Can I assist you with something?
Yes, please. Where is the bank located?
It's just around the corner. See you later!
Thank you! Goodbye!
Have a good day!
Good evening! Good night!

Phase No. 2

Continue in the same way for the following lessons. For example, for lesson No. 8, first translate the text of lesson No. 8 from the target language into English, then translate the text of lesson No. 2 from English back into the target language, and so on.

Additionally, every 10 lessons, a small challenge awaits you to put your knowledge into practice.

Note: Your translations do not need to match the manual texts perfectly, but they should convey a similar meaning. If you are using the paper version of the manual, note your translations directly at the bottom of the text, or else use a separate notebook.

AND WHAT ABOUT GRAMMAR?

You've probably been told that mastering a language starts with grammar. But this traditional approach is not only discouraging, it's also counterproductive. Learning a language is really about diving into a living world and understanding how words and sentences come to life in real situations, not by endlessly reciting rules.

One of the biggest mistakes many learners make is trying to memorize grammar rules by heart. It's tedious, demotivating, and ineffective. Why? Because our brains remember things that make sense and are used regularly. Rules without context are quickly forgotten. It's disconnected from real-life learning: instead of speaking, feeling, and immersing yourself in the language, you end up drowning in sterile theories.

We strongly believe that grammar shouldn't be learned before using a language, but rather through natural usage.

Our method is based on a simple principle: start by using the language, then adjust your understanding of grammar as it comes up in real-life situations. You learn to speak and understand, just like a child discovering their native language. When a grammar question arises, you find the answer and remember it because it's relevant at that moment.

How does it work in practice?

1. Immerse yourself in the language without worrying about grammar rules at first.
2. When a grammar question naturally comes up ("Why is this word used here?"), look for the answer.
3. Write down the grammar points you come across on a separate page or in the blank section of this manual, like a grammar journal.
4. Keep repeating this process, question after question, and watch how your understanding grows without feeling like you're studying.

By using this method, you'll see real results: each grammar point is anchored in a real context, making it easier to remember and longer-lasting. Instead of getting stuck in grammar books, you'll be using the language right away, gaining confidence and fluency in your communication. Plus, you'll enjoy it more—learning becomes an exciting journey where each discovery is a personal victory.

Grammar will become an ally, not a hurdle, helping you progress naturally and smoothly.

With Natura Lingua, you're not following a rigid method—you're living the language. Grammar is no longer a mountain to climb, but a natural path that unfolds as you go, step by step.

ADDITIONAL RESOURCES

DOWNLOAD THE RESOURCES ASSOCIATED WITH THIS MANUAL AND GREATLY ENHANCE YOUR CHANCES OF SUCCESS.

Scan this QR code to access them:

SCAN ME

☞ **https://www.natura-lingua.com/download**

• **Optimize your learning with audio:** To significantly improve your language skills, we strongly advise you to download the audio files accompanying this manual. This will enhance your listening comprehension and pronunciation.

• **Enhance your learning with flashcards:** Flashcards are excellent tools for vocabulary memorization. We highly encourage you to use them to maximize your results. Download our set of cards, specially designed for this manual.

• **Join our learning community:** If you're looking to connect with other language enthusiasts through "Natura Lingua", we invite you to join our online group. In this community, you'll have the opportunity to ask questions, find learning partners, and share your progress.

• **Explore more with other Natura Lingua manuals:** If you like this method, note that there are other similar manuals for different languages. Discover our complete collection of manuals to enrich your linguistic learning experience in a natural and progressive way.

We are here to support you in learning the target language. For optimal results, we highly recommend downloading the audio and using the flashcards. These additional resources are designed to further facilitate your journey.

Happy learning!

MODERN GREEK IN 100 DAYS

Check off a box below after completing each lesson. This will aid you in monitoring your progress and maintaining motivation throughout your learning experience.

IMPORTANT NOTES :

1. **The Essentials: Vocabulary and Key Phrases:** In each Natura Lingua lesson, we carefully select the most useful words and expressions relevant to the theme studied. The goal is to familiarize you with the most frequently used constructions in the target language. Sometimes, the general meaning of the texts might seem surprising, but don't worry, it's an essential part of our method. It helps you focus on the practical aspects of the language, thereby accelerating your learning for better understanding and more effective communication.

2. **Translation: As Close to the Original as Possible:** We translate in a way that stays true to the source text, capturing how sentences are structured and ideas are conveyed in the target language. Our goal is not syntactic perfection in English, but rather to give you an authentic insight into the thought process and structure of the language you are learning. This method immerses you in the language, allowing you to gain a more natural and intuitive understanding. Our aim is to help you think and communicate fluently in the learned language, not just understand it. We want to prepare you to use the language practically and confidently in your daily life.

1. **Καλημέρα!**
2. **Καλημέρα**, πώς είσαι;
3. Καλά, ευχαριστώ. Και εσύ;
4. Επίσης καλά, **ευχαριστώ.**
5. **Καλό απόγευμα** πλέον, έτσι δεν είναι;
6. Ναι, **καλό απόγευμα!** Θα πάμε για καφέ;
7. Με χαρά.
8. **Καλησπέρα** στον καφέ τότε.
9. **Καληνύχτα** και **τα λέμε αργότερα.**

✤ In Greek, nouns have genders, so the word for "hello" changes from "γεια σου" to "γεια σας" depending on if you're speaking to one person or many.

DAY 1: GREETINGS

1. **Good morning**!
2. **Good morning**, how are you?
3. Good, thank you. And you?
4. Also good, **thank you**.
5. **Good afternoon** now, isn't it?
6. Yes, **good afternoon**! Shall we go for coffee?
7. With pleasure.
8. **Good evening** at the cafe then.
9. **Good night** and **talk to you later**.

✤ In Greece, it's common to greet friends with a warm embrace and two kisses, one on each cheek.

1. Καλημέρα, θέλεις καφέ;
2. **Ναι**, παρακαλώ.
3. **Μικρός** ή **μεγάλος**;
4. **Μεγάλος**, ευχαριστώ.
5. **Εντάξει**. Θέλεις κάτι άλλο;
6. **Ίσως** νερό.
7. **Συγγνώμη**, δεν έχουμε νερό.
8. **Λυπάμαι, όχι** πρόβλημα.
9. Καληνύχτα.

✤ In Greek, verbs change form to match the subject in both number and person.

DAY 2: COMMON EXPRESSIONS

1. Good morning, would you like some coffee?
2. **Yes**, please.
3. **Small** or **large**?
4. **Large**, thank you.
5. **Okay**. Would you like anything else?
6. **Maybe** some water.
7. **Sorry**, we don't have water.
8. **I'm sorry**, **no** problem.
9. Good night.

♣ In Greece, saying 'you're writing with a golden pen' means you're speaking highly of someone, originating from ancient times when important texts were written with golden ink.

ΗΜΈΡΑ ΝΟΎΜΕΡΟ 3: ΛΕΞΙΛΌΓΙΟ ΠΑΡΟΥΣΊΑΣΗΣ

1. **Γεια σας! Είμαι άνδρας.**
2. **Γεια σας! Είμαι γυναίκα. Πώς είστε;**
3. **Είμαι καλά, ευχαριστώ! Εσείς;**
4. **Είμαι καλά επίσης, ευχαριστώ. Πώς σας λένε;**
5. **Με λένε Γιώργο. Και εσάς;**
6. **Με λένε Μαρία. Πόσο χρονών είστε;**
7. **Είμαι 30 χρονών. Εσείς;**
8. **Είμαι 28 χρονών.**
9. **Εντάξει, χάρηκα πολύ.**

✤ In Modern Greek, adjectives agree with the nouns they describe in gender, number, and case.

DAY 3: INTRODUCTION VOCABULARY

1. Hello! I am a man.
2. Hello! I am a woman. How are you?
3. I am fine, thank you! And you?
4. I am also fine, thank you. What is your name?
5. My name is George. And yours?
6. My name is Maria. How old are you?
7. I am 30 years old. And you?
8. I am 28 years old.
9. Okay, it was very nice to meet you.

❖ In Greece, it's customary to offer guests a spoonful of sweet preserves, known as "spoon sweets," as a gesture of hospitality during local presentations.

ΗΜΈΡΑ ΝΟΎΜΕΡΟ 4: ΠΡΟΣΩΠΙΚΉ ΠΛΗΡΟΦΟΡΊΑ

1. Από πού είσαι;
2. Είμαι από την Ελλάδα. Εσείς;
3. Μένω στην Ιταλία.
4. Τι κάνεις στη ζωή σου;
5. Είμαι δάσκαλος. Και εσύ;
6. Είμαι φοιτητής. Τι σου αρέσει;
7. Μου αρέσει η μουσική και ο αθλητισμός.
8. Χάρηκα για τη γνωριμία!
9. Καλή μέρα και ευχαριστώ!

✤ In Greek, the definite article changes form to match the gender, number, and case of the noun it describes.

1. Where are you from?
2. I'm from Greece. And you?
3. I live in Italy.
4. What do you do for a living?
5. I'm a teacher. And you?
6. I'm a student. What do you like?
7. I like music and sports.
8. Nice to meet you!
9. Have a good day and thank you!

✤ In Greece, it's common to exchange personal visiting cards during social and business meetings as a gesture of goodwill and networking.

1. Καλή μέρα! **Καταλαβαίνω** ότι είσαι νέος εδώ.
2. Ναι, μόλις **ήρθα. Χρειάζομαι** να βρω ένα μέρος για να μείνω.
3. Έχω έναν φίλο που **μπορεί** να σε βοηθήσει. **Ξέρω** ότι **έχει** ένα διαμέρισμα.
4. Αλήθεια; Θα **ήθελα** να το **δω. Μπορείς να μου δώσεις** την διεύθυνση;
5. Φυσικά, θα στο **δώσω** τώρα. **Πάω** να το **πάρω** από το σπίτι μου.
6. Ευχαριστώ πολύ! **Ανυπομονώ** να μετακομίσω.
7. Εντάξει, **θα πάω** να το **πάρω. Συγγνώμη**, πρέπει να φύγω τώρα.
8. Κανένα πρόβλημα. Σε ευχαριστώ πάλι.
9. Καλή τύχη! Και καλή μέρα.

✤ In Greek, the indefinite article changes form based on the gender, number, and case of the noun it accompanies, for example, "ένας" for masculine, "μία" or "μια" for feminine, and "ένα" for neuter nouns.

1. Good day! **I understand** that you are new here.
2. Yes, I just **arrived**. **I need** to find a place to stay.
3. **I have** a friend who **can** help you. **I know** he **has** an apartment.
4. Really? I would **like** to **see** it. **Can you** give me the address?
5. Of course, I will **give** it to you now. **I am going** to **get** it from my house.
6. Thank you so much! **I am looking forward** to moving.
7. Okay, **I will go** to **get** it. **Sorry**, I have to leave now.
8. No problem. Thank you again.
9. Good luck! And have a good day.

✤ In Modern Greek, the verb "to have" (έχω) is used to express age, showing that age is perceived as something one possesses.

1. Θέλεις **καφέ** ή **τσάι**;
2. Προτιμώ **τσάι**, ευχαριστώ! Εσύ;
3. Εγώ θα πιω **καφέ**. Έχεις **γάλα**;
4. Ναι, έχω **γάλα** και **ζάχαρη**. Θέλεις;
5. Όχι, ευχαριστώ. Πίνω τον **καφέ** μου μαύρο.
6. Και το απόγευμα, τι πίνετε; **Μπύρα** ή **κρασί**;
7. Προτιμώ **νερό** ή κάποιο **αναψυκτικό**. Και εσύ;
8. Μου αρέσει ένα ποτήρι **κρασί**. Είναι ωραίο για το δείπνο.
9. Καταλαβαίνω. Καλή ιδέα!

✤ In Greek, the pronoun changes form to match the gender of the beverage, like "αυτός" for masculine, "αυτή" for feminine, and "αυτό" for neuter.

1. Do you want **coffee** or **tea**?
2. I prefer **tea**, thank you! And you?
3. I'll have **coffee**. Do you have **milk**?
4. Yes, I have **milk** and **sugar**. Would you like some?
5. No, thank you. I drink my **coffee** black.
6. And in the evening, what do you drink? **Beer** or **wine**?
7. I prefer **water** or some **soft drink**. And you?
8. I like a glass of **wine**. It's nice for dinner.
9. I understand. Good idea!

✤ In Greece, sharing a bottle of Ouzo symbolizes friendship and unity, often accompanied by lively discussions and laughter.

Important Reminder Before Starting Lesson 7

* * *

Congratulations on your progress so far! You are about to embark on a crucial stage of your learning: Phase No. 2.

Please follow these instructions starting from lesson 7:

- For each lesson from No. 7 onward, first translate the text of that lesson (No. 7, No. 8, etc.) from the target language into English.
- Then, go back 6 lessons and translate the English version of that lesson's text from English back into the target language, without referring to the original text.
- Compare your translation with the original text of that lesson and adjust if necessary.
- Read the original text of that lesson out loud, while listening to the audio.

This new phase is designed to activate the vocabulary you have already assimilated. Keep up the momentum and enjoy this enriching new phase of your learning!

ΗΜΈΡΑ ΑΡΙΘ. 7: ΠΕΡΙΓΡΑΦΙΚΆ ΕΠΊΘΕΤΑ Ι

1. Καλή μέρα! Από πού είσαι;
2. Είμαι από την Αθήνα. Εσύ;
3. Μένω στη Θεσσαλονίκη. Τι κάνεις στη ζωή σου;
4. Είμαι δάσκαλος. Και εσύ;
5. Είμαι φοιτητής. Τι σου αρέσει;
6. Μου αρέσει η μουσική και ο αθλητισμός. Θέλεις έναν καφέ;
7. Όχι, ευχαριστώ. Προτιμώ ένα **κρύο** νερό. Ο καφές είναι πολύ **ζεστός** για μένα.
8. Καταλαβαίνω. Έχω ένα **καινούργιο** αναψυκτικό. Θέλεις;
9. Ναι, θα ήθελα. Ευχαριστώ! **Χάρηκα για τη γνωριμία!**

❖ In Greek, adjectives can become adverbs by adding -α (for example, "γρήγορος" for "fast" becomes "γρήγορα" to mean "quickly").

1. Good day! Where are you from?
2. I'm from Athens. You?
3. I live in Thessaloniki. What do you do for a living?
4. I'm a teacher. And you?
5. I'm a student. What do you like?
6. I like music and sports. Would you like a coffee?
7. No, thank you. I prefer a **cold** water. Coffee is too **hot** for me.
8. I understand. I have a **new** soda. Would you like it?
9. Yes, I would like that. Thank you! **Nice to meet you!**

✤ In Modern Greek literature, the adjective "φωτεινός" (bright) is often used metaphorically to describe not just physical light, but the illumination of the mind and spirit.

ΗΜΈΡΑ ΝΟΎΜΕΡΟ 8: ΤΟΠΟΘΕΣΊΑ ΚΑΙ ΚΑΤΕΥΘΎΝΣΕΙΣ I 🌱

1. Πού είναι το μουσείο; Είναι **κοντά**;
2. Ναι, είναι **κοντά**. Πρέπει να πας **ευθεία** και μετά **δεξιά**.
3. **Από εδώ ή από εκεί**;
4. **Από εδώ, ευθεία** και μετά **δεξιά**.
5. Είναι **μακριά από εκεί**;
6. Όχι, δεν είναι **μακριά**. Είναι πολύ **κοντά**.
7. Καταλαβαίνω. Ευχαριστώ πολύ.
8. Παρακαλώ. Καλή επίσκεψη στο μουσείο!

✤ In Modern Greek, to express location, we often use the preposition "σε" (in, at) followed by the definite article, like in "στο σπαρταριστό πάρκο" (in the bustling park).

54

1. Where is the museum? Is it **close**?
2. Yes, it's **close**. You need to go **straight** and then **right**.
3. **From here or from there**?
4. **From here**, **straight** and then **right**.
5. Is it **far from there**?
6. No, it's not **far**. It's very **close**.
7. I understand. Thank you very much.
8. You're welcome. Enjoy your visit to the museum!

✤ The Acropolis of Athens, a symbol of classical spirit and civilization, hosts the Panathenaic Festival every four years, celebrating Athena's birthday with both ancient and modern Greeks.

1. **Στρίψτε αριστερά** εδώ ή **δεξιά**;
2. **Αριστερά. Το καφέ είναι πάνω από** την τράπεζα.
3. Και **πίσω** από το καφέ, τι υπάρχει;
4. Ένα πάρκο. Αλλά **δίπλα** στο καφέ υπάρχει ένα μπαρ.
5. Θέλετε να πάμε **πάνω** στο μπαρ για μία μπύρα;
6. Όχι, προτιμώ καφέ. **Σταματήστε εδώ**. Θα πιούμε καφέ.
7. Εντάξει, **κάτω** από τον ήλιο είναι ωραία.

✤ In Greek, to combine directions or locations, use the conjunction "και" (and) for adding or "ή" (or) for options.

1. **Turn left** here or **right**?
2. **Left. The café is above** the bank.
3. And **behind** the café, what is there?
4. A park. But **next to** the café there is a bar.
5. Do you want to go **up** to the bar for a beer?
6. No, I prefer coffee. **Stop here**. We'll have coffee.
7. Okay, **under** the sun it's nice.

✤ In Athens, the Acropolis is guarded by stray cats, considered the modern guardians of ancient ruins.

1. **Πού** είναι το βιβλίο μου;
2. Είναι **πάνω** στο τραπέζι.
3. **Γιατί** είναι εκεί;
4. Επειδή εκεί το άφησες.
5. **Τι** ώρα είναι;
6. Είναι τέσσερις το απόγευμα.
7. **Πόσο κοστίζει** αυτό το παγωτό;
8. Κοστίζει τρία ευρώ.
9. **Πώς** θα πάω στην πλατεία;
10. Πρέπει να πας **αριστερά** και μετά **δεξιά**.

✤ In Greek, to form a question, you can simply add the interjection "έ;" at the end of a statement.

1. **Where** is my book?
2. It's **on** the table.
3. **Why** is it there?
4. Because that's where you left it.
5. **What** time is it?
6. It's four in the afternoon.
7. **How much** does this ice cream cost?
8. It costs three euros.
9. **How** do I get to the square?
10. You need to go **left** and then **right**.

✤ In Modern Greek culture, asking direct questions is often seen as a sign of genuine interest and care, rather than prying.

CHALLENGE NO. 1

CHOOSE A THEME AND CREATE A COLLAGE
OF PHOTOS OR IMAGES, NOTING THE
CORRESPONDING WORD IN MODERN
GREEK.

"Η επιμονή είναι ο κλειδί της επιτυχίας."

"Perseverance is the key to success."

1. **Τώρα** είναι η **ώρα** να μάθουμε.
2. **Σήμερα**; Γιατί όχι **αύριο**;
3. **Χθες ήταν πολύ αργά. Και μεθαύριο** θα είναι πολύ αργά.
4. Πότε ξεκινάμε;
5. **Τώρα**. Κάθε **δευτερόλεπτο** μετράει.
6. Πώς θα το κάνουμε;
7. Απλά. Ένα **λεπτό** κάθε **ημέρα**.
8. Και πού;
9. Εδώ, αριστερά από το δωμάτιο.

❖ In Greek, to say "It is 3 o'clock," you use "Είναι οι τρεις."

DAY 11: DAYS AND TIME

1. **Now** is the time to learn.
2. **Today**? Why not **tomorrow**?
3. **Yesterday was too late. And the day after tomorrow** will be too late.
4. When do we start?
5. **Now**. Every **second** counts.
6. How will we do it?
7. Simply. One **minute** every **day**.
8. And where?
9. Here, to the left of the room.

✤ In Modern Greek culture, the concept of "siga siga" (slowly, slowly) reflects a relaxed approach to time, emphasizing living in the moment and not rushing life.

ΗΜΈΡΑ ΝΟΎΜΕΡΟ 12: ΗΜΈΡΕΣ ΤΗΣ ΕΒΔΟΜΆΔΑΣ

1. **Τι μέρα είναι σήμερα;**
2. **Σήμερα είναι Πέμπτη.**
3. Και **αύριο**;
4. **Αύριο είναι Παρασκευή.**
5. Ωραία! Και **μεθαύριο**;
6. **Μεθαύριο είναι Σάββατο. Έχουμε σαββατοκύριακο.**
7. Εντάξει, ευχαριστώ.
8. Όχι πρόβλημα.

❖ In Greek, the days of the week are always written with a lowercase letter and they act as the subject in sentences like "Τρίτη είναι ημέρα εργασίας" (Tuesday is a workday).

DAY 12: DAYS OF THE WEEK

1. **What day is it today?**
2. **Today is Thursday.**
3. And **tomorrow?**
4. **Tomorrow is Friday.**
5. Great! And **the day after tomorrow?**
6. **The day after tomorrow is Saturday. We have a weekend.**
7. Okay, thank you.
8. No problem.

✤ In Modern Greek, the days of the week are named after the Sun, the Moon, and the five known planets of antiquity, reflecting ancient astrological traditions.

1. Είμαι η **μητέρα** σας.
2. Ευχαριστούμε, **μητέρα**!
3. Και εγώ ο **πατέρας**.
4. Πού είναι οι **παππούδες**;
5. Στο σπίτι τους.
6. Εμείς, οι **γονείς**, πάμε εκεί την Παρασκευή.
7. Γιατί;
8. Για να τους δούμε.
9. Εσείς, τα **παιδιά**, θέλετε να έρθετε;

✤ In Greek, to show the direct object of a verb, we often use the accusative case, adding specific endings to nouns and pronouns.

DAY 13: FAMILY I

1. I am your **mother**.
2. Thank you, **mother**!
3. And I am the **father**.
4. Where are the **grandparents**?
5. At their house.
6. We, the **parents**, are going there on Friday.
7. Why?
8. To see them.
9. You, the **children**, want to come?

❖ In Modern Greek families, it's common for multiple generations to live under one roof, fostering a strong sense of community and support.

ΗΜΈΡΑ ΝΟΎΜΕΡΟ 14: ΟΙΚΟΓΈΝΕΙΑ ΙΙ ⚘

1. Χαίρετε, είμαι ο **ξάδερφός** σας.
2. Χαίρομαι πολύ! Εγώ είμαι η **θεία** σας.
3. Και εγώ ο **θείος**. Πώς είναι οι **φίλοι** σας;
4. Είναι καλά, ευχαριστώ. Και ο **συνάδελφός** μου είναι εδώ.
5. Πού μένετε τώρα;
6. Μένω στην Αθήνα. Και εσείς;
7. Εμείς μένουμε κοντά εδώ. Τι κάνετε στη ζωή σας;
8. Είμαι δάσκαλος. Μου αρέσει η μουσική.
9. Χάρηκα για τη γνωριμία! Καλή μέρα.

✤ In Greek, to show the indirect object, we often use the preposition "σε" before the noun, like in "Δίνω ένα δώρο στη μητέρα μου" (I give a gift to my mother).

1. Hello, I am your **cousin**.
2. Nice to meet you! I am your **aunt**.
3. And I am the **uncle**. How are your **friends**?
4. They are fine, thank you. And my **colleague** is here too.
5. Where do you live now?
6. I live in Athens. And you?
7. We live close by. What do you do for a living?
8. I am a teacher. I like music.
9. Nice to meet you! Have a good day.

✤ In Greece, name days are celebrated more grandly than birthdays, often with open houses and feasts.

1. Πόσους ξαδέρφους έχεις;
2. **Έχω** τρεις ξαδέρφους και **δύο** ξαδέρφες.
3. Και πόσους θείους;
4. **Έχω ένα** θείο και **μία** θεία.
5. Πότε πας στη θεία σου;
6. **Πάω** την **Παρασκευή**.
7. Καταλαβαίνεις τα μαθήματα στο σχολείο;
8. Ναι, **καταλαβαίνω**. **Ξέρω από ένα έως δέκα** στα αγγλικά.
9. Πολύ καλά!

❖ In Greek, when using numbers from 1 to 10 with verbs in the present tense, the verb agrees in number with the noun it refers to, not the numeral itself.

DAY 15: NUMBERS FROM 1 TO 10

1. How many cousins do you have?
2. **I have** three male cousins and **two** female cousins.
3. And how many uncles?
4. **I have one** uncle and **one** aunt.
5. When do you go to your aunt's?
6. **I go** on **Friday**.
7. Do you understand the lessons at school?
8. Yes, **I understand. I know from one to ten** in English.
9. Very good!

✤ In Modern Greek culture, the number 13 is considered lucky, contrary to many Western superstitions.

1. Μητέρα, πόσα μέλη έχει η οικογένειά μας;
2. **Δεκαπέντε**, αγάπη μου.
3. Και πόσα αναψυκτικά πρέπει να αγοράσουμε για το πάρτι;
4. **Είκοσι**, για να έχουμε κάποια επιπλέον.
5. Θέλει κανείς **καφέ** ή **τσάι** το πρωί;
6. Εγώ θα πάρω **καφέ**, μητέρα.
7. Και εγώ **τσάι**, παρακαλώ.
8. Ο πατέρας και ο αδελφός σου;
9. **Μπύρα** για τον πατέρα και **νερό** για τον αδελφό.

✤ In Greek, numbers from 11 to 19 are formed by adding the word "δέκα" (deka, meaning ten) after the unit number, except for 11 and 12 which are "έντεκα" (endeka) and "δώδεκα" (dodeka).

1. Mother, how many members are in our family?
2. **Fifteen**, my love.
3. And how many soft drinks should we buy for the party?
4. **Twenty**, so we have some extra.
5. Does anyone want **coffee** or **tea** in the morning?
6. I'll have **coffee**, mother.
7. And I'll have **tea**, please.
8. What about your father and brother?
9. **Beer** for dad and **water** for my brother.

✤ In Modern Greek culture, the game "Παίζω με τους αριθμούς" (Playing with Numbers) is not only a fun pastime but also a traditional way to teach children about mathematics and rhyming.

ΗΜΈΡΑ ΝΟΎΜΕΡΟ 17: ΨΏΝΙΑ I

1. Πάμε στην **αγορά**;
2. Ναι, χρειάζομαι πράγματα από το **κατάστημα**.
3. Θα **αγοράσω** μια μπλούζα.
4. Εγώ θα **κοιτάζω** παπούτσια. Είναι **ακριβά**;
5. Κάποια είναι, αλλά υπάρχει **εκπτωτική περίοδος** τώρα.
6. Ωραία! Θα βρω κάτι **φθηνό** με **έκπτωση**.
7. Πληρώνεις με **μετρητά** ή **πιστωτική κάρτα**;
8. Με πιστωτική κάρτα. Είναι πιο **γρήγορο**.

✣ In Modern Greek, to make a sentence negative, place "δεν" before the verb.

1. Shall we go to the **market**?
2. Yes, I need things from the **store**.
3. I will **buy** a shirt.
4. I will **look** at shoes. Are they **expensive**?
5. Some are, but there is a **discount period** now.
6. Great! I will find something **cheap** with a **discount**.
7. Do you pay with **cash** or **credit card**?
8. With a credit card. It's faster.

✤ In traditional Greek markets, it's common to haggle over prices, a practice known as "pechnidi," reflecting the lively art of negotiation deeply rooted in Greek culture.

1. Θέλω να αγοράσω **ρούχα** και **γυαλιά ηλίου**. Πού είναι το **δοκιμαστήριο**;
2. Είναι εκεί, δεξιά από το **ταμείο**.
3. Κοιτάζω την **τιμή**. Αυτό το **μπουφάν** είναι πολύ ακριβό.
4. Ναι, αλλά τα **κοσμήματα** εδώ είναι φθηνά. Θέλεις να δεις;
5. Μπορούμε να πάρουμε ένα **καλάθι** ή **καρότσι**;
6. Πάρε ένα **καλάθι**. Είναι εκεί, αριστερά.
7. Ευχαριστώ. Πάμε στο **ταμείο** για την **απόδειξη**.

✤ To form a question in Greek about shopping, simply place the verb at the beginning of the sentence and use a rising intonation.

1. I want to buy **clothes** and **sunglasses**. Where is the **fitting room**?
2. It's over there, to the right of the **cash register**.
3. I'm looking at the **price**. This **jacket** is very expensive.
4. Yes, but the **jewelry** here is cheap. Do you want to see?
5. Can we get a **basket** or **cart**?
6. Take a **basket**. It's over there, on the left.
7. Thank you. Let's go to the **cash register** for the **receipt**.

✤ In Greece, the world's oldest shopping mall was discovered in the ruins of Argilos, dating back to the 6th century BC, showcasing ancient Greek innovation in commerce.

1. Θέλω να πάω στο **αεροδρόμιο**. Ποιο **λεωφορείο** πρέπει να πάρω;
2. Πάρε το **λεωφορείο δεκαπέντε** που πάει **αριστερά** από τον **σταθμό**.
3. Και πόσο κοστίζει το εισιτήριο για το **αεροδρόμιο**;
4. Κοστίζει δέκα ευρώ. Μπορείς να πληρώσεις στο **ταμείο**.
5. Ευχαριστώ! Και αν θέλω να πάω με **ταξί**;
6. Το **ταξί** θα κοστίσει περίπου είκοσι ευρώ. Είναι πιο γρήγορο αλλά πιο ακριβό.
7. Καταλαβαίνω. Ίσως να προτιμήσω το **λεωφορείο** τελικά.
8. Καλή ιδέα. Είναι πιο οικονομικό και άνετο για το **αεροδρόμιο**.

✤ In Greek, to form a simple declarative sentence about transport, you start with the subject, followed by the verb, and then the means of transport, for example, "Εγώ πηγαίνω με το αυτοκίνητο" (I go by car).

1. I want to go to the **airport**. Which **bus** should I take?
2. Take the **bus fifteen** that goes **left** from the **station**.
3. And how much does the ticket to the **airport** cost?
4. It costs ten euros. You can pay at the **ticket office**.
5. Thank you! And if I want to go by **taxi**?
6. The **taxi** will cost about twenty euros. It's faster but more expensive.
7. I understand. I might prefer the **bus** after all.
8. Good idea. It's more economical and comfortable for the **airport**.

✤ In Greece, donkeys are still a popular mode of transportation on many of the islands, charmingly blending tradition with modern tourism.

1. Έχεις το **εισιτήριο** σου;
2. Ναι, και την **κάρτα επιβίβασης**. Πότε είναι η **αναχώρηση**;
3. Σε μία ώρα. Πρέπει να πάμε στον **τερματικό** σταθμό.
4. Από ποια **πύλη** φεύγει το αεροπλάνο;
5. Πύλη 5. Έχεις τις **αποσκευές** σου;
6. Μόνο μία **βαλίτσα** και ένα **σακίδιο πλάτης**.
7. Καλά, ας ελπίσουμε να μην είναι **καθυστερημένο** το αεροπλάνο.

✤ In Greek, to form an interrogative sentence about transport, start with the question word "Πώς" (How) followed by the verb and then the mode of transport, for example, "Πώς πάμε στο αεροδρόμιο με το λεωφορείο;" (How do we go to the airport by bus?).

DAY 20: TRANSPORT II 🌱

1. Do you have your **ticket**?
2. Yes, and the **boarding pass**. When is the **departure**?
3. In an hour. We need to go to the **terminal**.
4. Which **gate** is the plane leaving from?
5. Gate 5. Do you have your **luggage**?
6. Just one **suitcase** and a **backpack**.
7. Good, let's hope the plane isn't **delayed**.

❖ In Athens, the Metro Line 1, also known as the Green Line, has been in operation since 1869, making it one of the oldest public transport systems in the world.

CHALLENGE NO. 2

WRITE A SHORT TEXT IN MODERN GREEK
INTRODUCING YOURSELF AND
EXPLAINING WHY YOU ARE LEARNING
THIS LANGUAGE.

"Η μάθηση είναι ένα ταξίδι που δεν τελειώνει ποτέ."

"Learning is a journey that never ends."

1. Πάμε **στο πάρκο** τώρα;
2. Όχι, πρέπει να πάω **στο γραφείο** και μετά **στο φαρμακείο.**
3. Αύριο, θέλεις να πάμε **στο εστιατόριο**;
4. Ναι, αλλά πρώτα πρέπει να περάσω από **την τράπεζα.**
5. Και μετά **στο εστιατόριο**;
6. Ακριβώς. Μετά **στο εστιατόριο** για δείπνο.
7. Ωραία, θα πάρω και **το σπίτι** μου τηλέφωνο να ενημερώσω.
8. Καλή ιδέα. Θα είναι μια όμορφη μέρα.

✣ To give directions in Greek using the imperative form, simply use the verb that corresponds to the action you want to be taken, like "Πάμε!" for "Let's go!"

1. Shall we go **to the park** now?
2. No, I need to go **to the office** and then **to the pharmacy**.
3. Tomorrow, do you want to go **to the restaurant**?
4. Yes, but first I need to stop by **the bank**.
5. And then **to the restaurant**?
6. Exactly. Then **to the restaurant** for dinner.
7. Great, I'll also call **my house** to let them know.
8. Good idea. It will be a beautiful day.

✤ Greece's Acropolis, a beacon of ancient civilization, is so iconic that it has its own dedicated museum at its foot.

1. Το **μεγάλο** σπίτι είναι **υψηλό** ή **χαμηλό**;
2. Είναι **υψηλό**. Και το σχολείο είναι **μεγάλο** αλλά **χαμηλό**.
3. Πόσο **μακρύς** είναι ο δρόμος για το φαρμακείο;
4. Είναι **μικρός**. Πολύ **γρήγορος** με το αυτοκίνητο.
5. Το λεωφορείο είναι **γρήγορο** ή **αργό**;
6. Συνήθως είναι **αργό** και **θορυβώδες**.
7. Ποια μέρα πάμε στο αεροδρόμιο;
8. Την Παρασκευή. Είναι **πλατύς** και **μακρύς** ο δρόμος.

❖ In Greek, to form an exclamatory sentence with an adjective, place "τι" before the adjective for emphasis, like "Τι όμορφη μέρα!" (What a beautiful day!).

DAY 22: ADJECTIVES II

1. Is the **big** house **tall** or **short**?
2. It is **tall**. And the school is **big** but **short**.
3. How **long** is the road to the pharmacy?
4. It is **short**. Very **quick** by car.
5. Is the bus **fast** or **slow**?
6. It is usually **slow** and **noisy**.
7. Which day are we going to the airport?
8. On Friday. The road is **wide** and **long**.

✤ In Greece, the breathtaking Samaria Gorge in Crete is one of Europe's longest canyons, attracting hikers from around the world.

1. Αυτή η βαλίτσα είναι πολύ **βαριά**. Μπορείς να με βοηθήσεις;
2. Φυσικά, η δική μου είναι αρκετά **ελαφριά**. Πού πάτε;
3. Πάμε στο **τερματικό** για την **αναχώρηση**. Η πτήση μας είναι σε μία ώρα.
4. Ελπίζω να είναι **ήρεμη** η πτήση. Δεν μου αρέσουν οι **σκληρές** πτήσεις.
5. Ναι, και εγώ. Προτιμώ **ζεστό** καιρό όταν φτάσουμε.
6. Έχετε τα **εισιτήρια** και τις **κάρτες επιβίβασης**;
7. Όλα **έτοιμα** και έτοιμα. Η **οικογένεια** μου είναι πολύ ενθουσιασμένη.
8. Καλό ταξίδι! Ελπίζω να είναι **απαλό** και χωρίς προβλήματα.
9. Ευχαριστώ πολύ! Καλή συνέχεια σε σένα.

✤ In Greek, to make an adjective negative, place "δεν" before the adjective.

88

1. This suitcase is very **heavy**. Can you help me?
2. Of course, mine is quite **light**. Where are you going?
3. We're heading to the **terminal** for our **departure**. Our flight is in an hour.
4. I hope it's a **smooth** flight. I don't like **turbulent** flights.
5. Yes, me too. I prefer **warm** weather when we arrive.
6. Do you have the **tickets** and **boarding passes**?
7. All **set** and ready. My **family** is very excited.
8. Have a good trip! I hope it's **gentle** and without any problems.
9. Thank you very much! All the best to you.

✤ Modern Greek poets often use vivid adjectives to capture the luminous colors of the Aegean Sea.

1. Τι **χρώμα** είναι το **σπίτι** σου;
2. Είναι **λευκό** με **μπλε** παράθυρα.
3. Και το **γραφείο**;
4. Το **γραφείο** μου είναι **κίτρινο**. Πολύ **ζεστό** χρώμα.
5. Έχεις **ροζ** δωμάτιο;
6. Όχι, αλλά η **ανιψιά** μου έχει ένα **ροζ** δωμάτιο. Είναι πολύ **απαλό**.
7. Και τι **χρώμα** είναι το **αυτοκίνητο**;
8. Είναι **καφέ**. Λίγο **σκληρό** χρώμα, αλλά μου αρέσει.
9. Ωραία! Μου αρέσουν τα **χρώματα** που επιλέγεις.

❖ In Modern Greek, the spelling of color adjectives changes to match the gender (masculine, feminine, neuter) and number (singular, plural) of the noun they describe.

1. What **color** is your **house**?
2. It's **white** with **blue** windows.
3. And the **office**?
4. My **office** is **yellow**. A very **warm** color.
5. Do you have a **pink** room?
6. No, but my **niece** has a **pink** room. It's very **soft**.
7. And what **color** is the **car**?
8. It's **brown**. A bit of a **harsh** color, but I like it.
9. Nice! I like the **colors** you choose.

✤ In Modern Greek culture, blue is believed to ward off the evil eye, which is why many buildings and boats are painted in this protective color.

ΗΜΈΡΑ ΝΟΎΜΕΡΟ 25: ΗΛΕΚΤΡΟΝΙΚΆ ΚΑΙ ΤΕΧΝΟΛΟΓΊΑ I ⚘

1. Γεια, έχεις **Ίντερνετ** στο **έξυπνο κινητό** σου;
2. Ναι, χρησιμοποιώ **Wi-Fi**. Και εσύ;
3. Χρησιμοποιώ **Wi-Fi** στον **φορητό υπολογιστή** μου. Στέλνω **ηλεκτρονικό ταχυδρομείο**.
4. Έχεις **εφαρμογή** για **κοινωνικά δίκτυα**;
5. Ναι, και **κατεβάζω** βίντεο. Και εσύ;
6. Χρησιμοποιώ τον **περιηγητή** για να διαβάσω νέα.
7. Ωραία. Αντίο!
8. Καληνύχτα!

✤ In Greek, always use a semicolon (;) instead of a question mark (?) at the end of a question.

DAY 25: ELECTRONICS AND TECHNOLOGY I

1. Hello, do you have **Internet** on your **smartphone**?
2. Yes, I use **Wi-Fi**. What about you?
3. I use **Wi-Fi** on my **laptop**. I'm sending an **email**.
4. Do you have an **app** for **social networks**?
5. Yes, and I **download** videos. What about you?
6. I use the **browser** to read news.
7. Nice. Goodbye!
8. Goodnight!

✤ The Greeks invented the first known analog computer, the Antikythera mechanism, over 2,000 years ago to predict astronomical positions and eclipses.

1. **Εντάξει**, ποιος είναι ο αγαπημένος σου **μήνας**;
2. Μου αρέσει ο **Μάιος**. Είναι τόσο **ζεστός** και **απαλός**.
3. Και εμένα! Αλλά μου αρέσει και ο **Σεπτέμβριος**. Είναι **ήρεμος**.
4. Πόσες **εποχές** έχουμε;
5. **Δώδεκα μήνες** και τέσσερις **εποχές**.
6. **Συγγνώμη**, εννοούσα πόσες **εποχές**.
7. Α, **τέσσερις**. **Κρύος Ιανουάριος, ζεστός Ιούλιος**.
8. **Εντάξει**, και ποια **εποχή** προτιμάς;
9. Το καλοκαίρι. Είναι πιο **ζεστό**.

✤ In Greek, to express the past tense for actions that happened in specific months or seasons, we add the past tense suffix to the verb, like in "Πήγα στη θάλασσα τον Ιούλιο" (I went to the sea in July).

1. **Okay**, what's your favorite **month**?
2. I like **May**. It's so **warm** and **gentle**.
3. Me too! But I also like **September**. It's **calm**.
4. How many **seasons** do we have?
5. **Twelve months** and four **seasons**.
6. **Sorry**, I meant how many **seasons**.
7. Oh, **four. Cold January, warm July**.
8. **Okay**, and which **season** do you prefer?
9. Summer. It's warmer.

✤ In Greece, the Anastenaria festival involves fire-walking rituals to honor Saints Constantine and Helen, blending ancient pagan practices with Orthodox Christianity.

ΗΜΈΡΑ ΝΟΎΜΕΡΟ 27: ΠΕΡΙΣΣΌΤΕΡΟΙ ΜΉΝΕΣ ΚΑΙ ΕΠΟΧΈΣ

1. Ποια είναι η **πρόγνωση** για τον **Νοέμβριο**;
2. Θα έχουμε **βροχή** και λίγη **ηλιοφάνεια**. Ο **χειμώνας** έρχεται.
3. Και στον **Δεκέμβριο**;
4. Περισσότερη **βροχή**. Το **κλίμα** γίνεται πιο κρύο.
5. Μου αρέσει η **άνοιξη** περισσότερο.
6. Εγώ προτιμώ το **καλοκαίρι**. Εσείς;
7. Είμαι περισσότερο για το **φθινόπωρο**. Ευχαριστώ!

✤ In Modern Greek, to form the future tense, we add the prefix "θα" before the verb.

1. What's the **forecast** for **November**?
2. We'll have **rain** and a bit of **sunshine**. **Winter** is coming.
3. And in **December**?
4. More **rain**. The **weather** gets colder.
5. I prefer **spring** more.
6. I favor **summer**. How about you?
7. I'm more for **autumn**. Thank you!

✤ In Greece, the first day of May is celebrated by gathering flowers and creating intricate wreaths to hang on doors, symbolizing the rebirth of nature.

1. Γεια σου! Πώς είσαι σήμερα;
2. Είμαι πολύ **ευτυχισμένη**! Και εσύ;
3. Λίγο **λυπημένος**, αλλά δεν πειράζει. Τι σε κάνει τόσο ευτυχισμένη;
4. Μόλις έμαθα ότι πέρασα τις εξετάσεις! Είμαι πολύ **περήφανη**.
5. Αυτό είναι φανταστικό! Είμαι **χαρούμενος** για σένα.
6. Ευχαριστώ πολύ! Και τι σε κάνει λυπημένο;
7. Αισθάνομαι λίγο **μόνος** τελευταία. Αλλά θα περάσει.
8. Αν θες να βγούμε κάποια στιγμή, θα χαρώ πολύ!
9. Θα ήταν υπέροχο. Ευχαριστώ, νιώθω ήδη καλύτερα!

✤ In Modern Greek, the indicative mood is used to express facts or beliefs about the present, past, or future.

1. Hello! How are you today?
2. I'm very **happy**! And you?
3. A bit **sad**, but it's okay. What makes you so happy?
4. I just found out I passed my exams! I'm very **proud**.
5. That's fantastic! I'm **happy** for you.
6. Thank you so much! And what makes you sad?
7. I've been feeling a bit **lonely** lately. But it will pass.
8. If you want to go out sometime, I would be very happy!
9. That would be wonderful. Thank you, I already feel better!

✤ In Modern Greek culture, the smashing of plates is a traditional expression of joy and celebration, not anger.

1. Γιατί είσαι τόσο **αγχωμένος**;
2. Έχω μια σημαντική συνέντευξη αύριο και **χρειάζομαι** να πάω στο **αεροδρόμιο** με το **αυτοκίνητο**.
3. Μην είσαι **ανήσυχος**. Ξέρω ότι θα τα πας καλά.
4. Είμαι λίγο **μπερδεμένος**. Και **φοβισμένος**.
5. **Αστειεύομαι! Είμαι ενθουσιασμένος για εσένα.** **Σ' αγαπώ και μου λείπεις** όταν δεν είσαι εδώ.
6. Ευχαριστώ, αισθάνομαι πιο **χαλαρός** τώρα. **Καταλαβαίνω** ότι πρέπει να είμαι πιο θετικός.

❖ In Greek, to give commands or make requests politely, we use the imperative mood, changing the verb ending according to the person you're speaking to.

1. Why are you so **stressed**?
2. I have an important interview tomorrow and **need** to go to the **airport** by **car**.
3. Don't be **worried. I know** you'll do well.
4. I'm a bit **confused**. And **scared**.
5. **Just kidding! I'm excited for you. I love you and miss you** when you're not here.
6. Thank you, I feel more **relaxed** now. **I understand** that I need to be more positive.

♣ In Modern Greek culture, the love poems of Nobel laureate Odysseas Elytis are often recited at weddings, symbolizing eternal love and the beauty of the Greek landscape.

1. Έχεις **πόνο** στο **κεφάλι**;
2. Ναι, και τα **μάτια** μου είναι **ανήσυχα**.
3. Πρέπει να πιεις λίγο **νερό**. Θέλεις;
4. Ευχαριστώ, αλλά προτιμώ ένα **τσάι**.
5. Έχεις **πυρετό**; Νιώθεις το **χέρι** σου ζεστό.
6. Όχι, απλά είμαι λίγο **αγχωμένος** για την **αναχώρηση** τον **Δεκέμβριο**.
7. Καταλαβαίνω. Θα περάσει. Κράτα το **αυτί** σου ανοιχτό για καλά νέα.
8. Ελπίζω. Τουλάχιστον δεν έχω **πόνο** στο **δόντι**.
9. Αυτό είναι καλό! Πάντα να βλέπεις το θετικό.

✤ In Greek, to express a wish or desire involving body parts, like "May your hands always be strong," we use the subjunctive mood by adding "να" before the verb.

1. Do you have **pain** in your **head**?
2. Yes, and my **eyes** are **restless**.
3. You should drink some **water**. Would you like some?
4. Thank you, but I'd prefer a **tea**.
5. Do you have a **fever**? Your **hand** feels warm.
6. No, I'm just a bit **stressed** about the **departure** in **December**.
7. I understand. It will pass. Keep your **ear** open for good news.
8. I hope so. At least I don't have **pain** in my **tooth**.
9. That's good! Always look on the bright side.

✤ In Modern Greek culture, the annual "Miss Hellas" beauty pageant is a celebrated event, showcasing diverse beauty standards that reflect the country's rich history and modern societal values.

CHALLENGE NO. 3

CHOOSE A SHORT ARTICLE IN A MODERN GREEK NEWSPAPER AND TRANSLATE IT INTO ENGLISH.

"Η καλή επικοινωνία είναι η γέφυρα προς την κατανόηση."

"Good communication is the bridge to understanding."

1. Έχω πόνο στο **γόνατο** και στην **πλάτη** μου.
2. Πρέπει να πας στο **νοσοκομείο** ή στο **φαρμακείο**.
3. Ναι, αλλά νιώθω και λίγο **λυπημένη**.
4. Μήπως έπεσες και χτύπησες το **κεφάλι** σου;
5. Όχι, αλλά έσκυψα γρήγορα και ένιωσα τον πόνο.
6. Ίσως να έχεις τεντώσει κάποιο **μυ** στη **πλάτη**.
7. Θα πάρω κάτι ζεστό να βάλω στο **γόνατο**.
8. Καλή ιδέα. Και μην ξεχάσεις να ξεκουραστείς.
9. Ευχαριστώ, θα προσπαθήσω να είμαι πιο **χαλαρή**.

✤ If you wanted to say "If I had strong legs, I would run faster" in Greek, you would use the conditional mood to express the hypothetical situation.

1. I have pain in my **knee** and in my **back**.
2. You should go to the **hospital** or to the **pharmacy**.
3. Yes, but I also feel a bit **sad**.
4. Did you fall and hit your **head**?
5. No, but I bent over quickly and felt the pain.
6. You might have strained a **muscle** in your **back**.
7. I'll get something warm to put on my **knee**.
8. Good idea. And don't forget to rest.
9. Thank you, I'll try to be more **relaxed**.

✤ In Greece, the dance of Zalongo is a poignant reminder of freedom, where women chose to dance off a cliff rather than be captured by Ottoman forces.

1. Ξέρεις ποια **ημέρα** είναι σήμερα;
2. Όχι, πρέπει να κοιτάξω το **ημερολόγιο**.
3. Είναι Τρίτη και έχουμε συνάντηση. Έχεις ετοιμάσει το **πρόγραμμα**;
4. Αχ, ξέχασα! Πόση **ώρα** έχουμε μέχρι τη συνάντηση;
5. Μόνο μισή **ώρα**. Πρέπει να βιαστούμε.
6. Και πόσες **ημέρες** έχουμε μέχρι το τέλος του **μήνα**;
7. Έχουμε ακόμα δύο **εβδομάδες**. Αλλά μην ανησυχείς, θα τα καταφέρουμε.
8. Ελπίζω το **έτος** αυτό να είναι καλύτερο από το προηγούμενο.
9. Σίγουρα θα είναι. Ας εργαστούμε σκληρά και όλα θα πάνε καλά.

✤ In Modern Greek, to express an action happening at a specific time, we use the active voice by placing the verb in the present, past, or future tense according to the time the action occurs.

1. Do you know what **day** it is today?
2. No, I need to check the **calendar**.
3. It's Tuesday, and we have a meeting. Have you prepared the **schedule**?
4. Oh, I forgot! How much **time** do we have until the meeting?
5. Only half an **hour**. We need to hurry.
6. And how many **days** do we have until the end of the **month**?
7. We still have two **weeks**. But don't worry, we'll manage.
8. I hope this **year** will be better than the last.
9. It definitely will be. Let's work hard and everything will be fine.

❖ In Greece, the traditional calendar was so integral to daily life that many villages had their own versions, aligning festivals and agricultural activities with local saints' days and natural cycles.

1. Θέλεις **καφέ** ή **τσάι** το πρωί;
2. Προτιμώ **καφέ**. Και εσύ;
3. Εγώ θα πάρω **τσάι**. Είναι πιο **ήρεμο** για το **κεφάλι** μου.
4. Καταλαβαίνω. Τι θα φάμε για πρωινό;
5. Έχω **αυγά, ψωμί και λίγα λαχανικά**.
6. Ας κάνουμε ομελέτα με **λαχανικά** και **ψωμί**. Τι λες;
7. Ναι, ακούγεται τέλειο. Έχεις **φρούτα**;
8. Έχω μπανάνες και μήλα. Θέλεις;
9. Μια μπανάνα θα ήταν ωραία. Ευχαριστώ.

❖ In Modern Greek, to form the passive voice for verbs related to food, we often add the suffix "-ται" to the verb root.

1. Do you want **coffee** or **tea** in the morning?
2. I prefer **coffee**. What about you?
3. I'll have **tea**. It's more **calming** for my **head**.
4. I understand. What shall we have for breakfast?
5. I have **eggs, bread, and some vegetables**.
6. Let's make an omelette with **vegetables** and **bread**. What do you say?
7. Yes, that sounds perfect. Do you have any **fruit**?
8. I have bananas and apples. Would you like some?
9. A banana would be nice. Thank you.

❖ Greece's moussaka, a rich layered dish, was popularized in the 1920s by chef Nikolaos Tselementes, who introduced béchamel sauce to traditional Greek cuisine.

1. Τι θα φάμε σήμερα;
2. Θέλω **κοτόπουλο** με **σαλάτα**.
3. Και για πρώτο;
4. Μια **σούπα** με λίγο **πιπέρι**.
5. Θέλεις κάτι να πιεις;
6. Ναι, ένα ποτήρι **νερό** και μετά **καφέ**.
7. Εγώ θα φτιάξω **σάντουιτς** με **τυρί** και **βούτυρο**.
8. Και για επιδόρπιο;
9. Ένα κομμάτι **κέικ**.

✤ In Greek, to express the circumstance of eating or drinking something, use the accusative case for the food or drink.

1. What are we eating today?
2. I want **chicken** with **salad**.
3. And for starters?
4. A **soup** with a bit of **pepper**.
5. Do you want something to drink?
6. Yes, a glass of **water** and then **coffee**.
7. I'll make a **sandwich** with **cheese** and **butter**.
8. And for dessert?
9. A piece of **cake**.

✤ In Greece, the beloved moussaka recipe was refined to its current form in the early 20th century by chef Nikolaos Tselementes, who introduced the béchamel sauce topping, blending French cuisine with traditional Greek ingredients.

1. Θέλεις **αναψυκτικό** ή **νερό**;
2. Προτιμώ **χυμό**. Και εσύ;
3. Εγώ θα πάρω **κρασί**. Και για επιδόρπιο;
4. Έχουν **παγωτό** και **σοκολάτα**.
5. Α, θα πάρω **παγωτό**. Και εσύ;
6. Μια **πίτα** θα ήταν τέλεια.
7. Καλή ιδέα! Θα πάρω και εγώ **πίτα**.
8. Τέλεια, ας παραγγείλουμε τώρα.
9. Ναι, ας το κάνουμε!

✤ In Greek, an independent clause can stand alone as a sentence, like "Πίνω καφέ" (I drink coffee) or "Τρώω γλυκό" (I eat dessert).

DAY 35: DRINKS AND DESSERTS

1. Do you want a **soda** or **water**?
2. I prefer **juice**. How about you?
3. I'll have **wine**. And for dessert?
4. They have **ice cream** and **chocolate**.
5. Ah, I'll take **ice cream**. And you?
6. A **pie** would be perfect.
7. Good idea! I'll have a **pie** too.
8. Great, let's order now.
9. Yes, let's do it!

❖ The beloved Greek dessert baklava was so coveted that it sparked a "baklava war" between Greece and Turkey, each claiming its origin.

1. Τι θα φτιάξουμε σήμερα στην κουζίνα;
2. Θέλω να κάνω **ψητό** κρέας.
3. Στον **φούρνο** ή **τηγανητό**;
4. **Ψημένο στον φούρνο**. Και θα προσθέσω λίγα λαχανικά.
5. Ωραία. Θα βάλω το κρέας στο **πιάτο** μετά.
6. Μην ξεχάσεις το **κουτάλι**, το **πηρούνι** και το **μαχαίρι**.
7. Φυσικά. Και τι θα πιούμε; **Κρασί** ή **νερό**;
8. Ας πιούμε λίγο **κρασί**. Ταιριάζει με το φαγητό.
9. Τέλεια. Όλα είναι έτοιμα για το δείπνο.

✤ In Greek, when describing a recipe, you use a subordinate clause to explain why or how something is done, starting with "που" (that) or "γιατί" (because).

1. What are we going to make in the kitchen today?
2. I want to make **roasted** meat.
3. In the **oven** or **fried**?
4. **Roasted in the oven**. And I'll add some vegetables.
5. Nice. I'll put the meat on the **plate** afterwards.
6. Don't forget the **spoon, fork, and knife**.
7. Of course. And what shall we drink; **wine** or **water**?
8. Let's have some **wine**. It goes well with the food.
9. Perfect. Everything is ready for dinner.

✤ Chef Diane Kochilas has played a pivotal role in popularizing Greek cuisine globally, turning traditional dishes into modern culinary trends.

1. Θέλεις να πάμε στην **παραλία** αυτό το **καλοκαίρι**;
2. Προτιμώ το **βουνό**. Είναι πιο δροσερό και έχει όμορφα **δάση**.
3. Μήπως να επισκεφτούμε ένα **νησί**; Έχουν όμορφες **κοιλάδες** και **θάλασσα**.
4. Καλή ιδέα! Μπορούμε να κάνουμε και εξερεύνηση στο **ποτάμι**.
5. Και μην ξεχνάς, το **καλοκαίρι** είναι τέλειο για τέτοια ταξίδια.
6. Ναι, και η **οικογένεια** μας θα απολαύσει τη φύση.
7. Ας οργανώσουμε το ταξίδι μας για **Ιούλιο** τότε.

✤ In Greek, to create a complex sentence about travel, use conjunctions like "που" (that/which) to connect an independent clause about a place with a dependent clause describing something about it, for example, "Επισκέφτηκα το νησί που ο ήλιος δύει μαγικά." (I visited the island where the sun sets magically).

1. Do you want to go to the **beach** this **summer**?
2. I prefer the **mountains**. It's cooler and has beautiful **forests**.
3. Maybe we should visit an **island**? They have beautiful **valleys** and **sea**.
4. Good idea! We can also explore the **river**.
5. And don't forget, **summer** is perfect for such trips.
6. Yes, and our **family** will enjoy nature.
7. Let's plan our trip for **July** then.

❖ Patrick Leigh Fermor, a British author and traveler, famously walked from the Hook of Holland to Constantinople, immersing himself deeply in the cultures along the way, including Greece, where he later became a key figure in the Cretan resistance during World War II.

1. **Βοήθεια! Φωτιά** στο δάσος!
2. Καλέστε **αστυνομία** και **πυροσβεστική** αμέσως.
3. Πονάω, έχω **τραύμα**. Χρειάζομαι **γιατρό**.
4. Θα σε πάω στο **νοσοκομείο**. Έχεις **αλλεργία** σε κάποιο **φάρμακο**;
5. Όχι, αλλά πρέπει να πάρω **χάπι** για τον πόνο.
6. Είσαι **χαρούμενος** που θα πάμε στον **γιατρό**;
7. Ναι, θέλω να αισθανθώ καλύτερα. Ευχαριστώ, **ξάδερφε**.
8. Μετά, θα πιούμε **νερό** και θα ηρεμήσουμε.
9. Ευχαριστώ, είσαι πολύ **χαλαρός**.

✤ In Greek, adjectives describing pain or feeling must agree in gender, number, and case with the noun they describe, like in "Πονάει η κεφαλή μου" (My head hurts), where "η κεφαλή" (the head) is feminine.

1. **Help**! **Fire** in the forest!
2. Call **police** and **fire department** immediately.
3. I'm in pain, I have a **wound**. I need a **doctor**.
4. I'll take you to the **hospital**. Do you have an **allergy** to any **medicine**?
5. No, but I need to take a **pill** for the pain.
6. Are you **happy** that we are going to the **doctor**?
7. Yes, I want to feel better. Thank you, **cousin**.
8. Afterwards, we'll drink **water** and calm down.
9. Thank you, you're very **relaxed**.

✤ In Greece, the island of Ikaria is renowned for its high number of centenarians, often attributed to its residents' diet and lifestyle, making it one of the world's Blue Zones where people live significantly longer.

1. Χθες, είδα **είκοσι ένα** πυροσβέστες να σβήνουν μια **φωτιά**.
2. Σοβαρά; Και κάλεσαν την **αστυνομία**;
3. Ναι, και **είκοσι δύο** αστυνομικοί ήρθαν γρήγορα.
4. Ω, καλά. Και τα άτομα που τραυματίστηκαν;
5. Μεταφέρθηκαν στο **νοσοκομείο**. **Είκοσι τρία άτομα χρειάστηκαν γιατρό**.
6. Αυτό είναι τρομακτικό. Πώς αισθάνεσαι τώρα;
7. Λίγο **ανήσυχος** και **φοβισμένος**. Αλλά, **είκοσι τέσσερα** αυτοκίνητα της αστυνομίας ακόμα είναι έξω.
8. Καλό είναι που είναι εκεί για βοήθεια. Θα πρέπει να προσπαθήσουμε να μείνουμε ήρεμοι.
9. Ναι, έχεις δίκιο. Ευτυχώς, όλοι στο σπίτι είναι καλά.

✤ In Greek, adjectives and nouns must agree in number, so when counting objects from 21 to 30, both the number and the noun it describes change form to match in gender and number.

1. Yesterday, I saw **twenty-one** firefighters putting out a **fire**.
2. Really? And did they call the **police**?
3. Yes, and **twenty-two** police officers arrived quickly.
4. Oh, good. And the people who were injured?
5. They were taken to the **hospital**. **Twenty-three people needed a doctor**.
6. That's terrifying. How are you feeling now?
7. A bit **anxious** and **scared**. But, **twenty-four** police cars are still outside.
8. It's good that they are there to help. We should try to stay calm.
9. Yes, you're right. Thankfully, everyone at home is okay.

✤ In Greece, the traditional lottery game "Lotto" has been a popular pastime since 1959, intertwining hope and superstition in Greek society.

ΗΜΈΡΑ ΝΟΎΜΕΡΟ 40: ΗΜΈΡΕΣ ΤΗΣ ΕΒΔΟΜΆΔΑΣ

1. **Χθες** ήταν **Πέμπτη**. Πήγαμε στην **παραλία**.
2. Α, ναι; Και **σήμερα** τι κάνουμε;
3. **Σήμερα** είναι **Παρασκευή**. Θα πάμε στο **βουνό**.
4. Ωραία! Και **αύριο, Σάββατο**;
5. **Αύριο** θα ξεκουραστούμε. Ίσως πάμε για περίπατο στο **δάσος**.
6. Και την **Κυριακή**;
7. Την **Κυριακή** θα επισκεφτούμε τη **θάλασσα** πάλι.

✤ In Greek, to compare days of the week, we use "πιο" (more) before the day for comparative, like "Σήμερα είναι πιο απασχολημένη από τη Δευτέρα" (Today is busier than Monday).

1. **Yesterday** was **Thursday**. We went to the **beach**.
2. Oh, really? And what are we doing **today**?
3. **Today is Friday. We're going to the mountain**.
4. Great! And **tomorrow, Saturday**?
5. **Tomorrow** we'll rest. Maybe we'll go for a walk in the **forest**.
6. And on **Sunday**?
7. On **Sunday**, we'll visit the **sea** again.

✤ In Modern Greek culture, it's considered unlucky to get a haircut on a Tuesday because it's believed to bring bad luck, stemming from the day's association with the god of war, Ares.

CHALLENGE NO. 4

WRITE A LETTER OR EMAIL IN MODERN GREEK TO A FICTIONAL OR REAL FRIEND.

Phrase: "Κάθε μέρα είναι μια ευκαιρία για να γίνεις καλύτερος."

"Every day is an opportunity to become better."

1. Σήμερα είναι Δευτέρα. Θα καθαρίσουμε τον **καναπέ** και το **τραπέζι**.
2. Και την **καρέκλα** και το **κρεβάτι**;
3. Ναι, και την **καρέκλα** και το **κρεβάτι**. Επίσης, το **μπάνιο** και την **κουζίνα**.
4. Θα καθαρίσουμε και την **λάμπα**, την **πόρτα**, το **παράθυρο** και τον **τοίχο**;
5. Φυσικά. Όλα πρέπει να είναι καθαρά.

✤ In Greek, to form the superlative of an adjective, you add "πιο" before the adjective for the comparative and "ο πιο" for the masculine, "η πιο" for the feminine, and "το πιο" for the neuter in the superlative, except for a few irregulars that change form.

1. Today is Monday. We will clean the **couch** and the **table**.
2. And the **chair** and the **bed**?
3. Yes, the **chair** and the **bed** too. Also, the **bathroom** and the **kitchen**.
4. Are we going to clean the **lamp**, the **door**, the **window**, and the **wall** as well?
5. Of course. Everything must be clean.

❖ In Modern Greek culture, the tradition of "Sarantaleitourgo" involves deep cleaning the house for 40 days before Easter to prepare for the holy celebration.

1. Έχουμε **σπίτι** με όμορφο **κήπο**.
2. Ναι, και το **διαμέρισμα** έχει ωραίο **μπαλκόνι**.
3. Πρέπει να καθαρίσουμε το **δωμάτιο** και το **μπάνιο** αυτή την **εβδομάδα**.
4. Και το **γκαράζ**; Είναι πολύ βρώμικο.
5. Ας καθαρίσουμε και το **δάπεδο** στο **γκαράζ**.
6. Θα αναλάβω εγώ το **καθάρισμα** της **σκάλας**.
7. Μην ξεχάσουμε το **μπαλκόνι**. Θέλει σκούπισμα.
8. Και τέλος, θα τακτοποιήσουμε τα έπιπλα, **καναπέ, τραπέζι, καρέκλα**.
9. Ωραία, θα έχουμε το **σπίτι** μας καθαρό μέχρι το τέλος της **εβδομάδας**.

❖ In Greek, to form the comparative degree of adjectives, you often add "-ότερος" for masculine and neuter, and "-ότερη" for feminine, after the adjective stem.

DAY 42: CLEANING II

1. We have a **house** with a beautiful **garden**.
2. Yes, and the **apartment** has a nice **balcony**.
3. We need to clean the **room** and the **bathroom** this **week**.
4. What about the **garage**? It's very dirty.
5. Let's also clean the **floor** in the **garage**.
6. I'll take care of cleaning the **stairs**.
7. Let's not forget the **balcony**. It needs sweeping.
8. And finally, we'll arrange the furniture, **sofa, table, chair**.
9. Great, our **house** will be clean by the end of the **week**.

✤ In Greece, the introduction of the refrigerator in households was so revolutionary that it sparked a cultural shift towards fresh food preservation, significantly reducing the reliance on salted and preserved meats.

1. Θέλεις να πάμε **δεξιά** στο **διαμέρισμα** για **καφέ**
   την **Πέμπτη**;
2. Ναι, αλλά προτιμώ **τσάι**. Είναι **δίπλα** στο **σταθμό**;
3. Όχι, είναι **ανάμεσα** στο **σουπερμάρκετ** και το
   φαρμακείο. Εδώ ή εκεί;
4. **Εδώ, μέσα στο κήπο. Έχει και λαχανικά.**
5. Ωραία, θα πάρουμε το **αυτοκίνητο** ή το
   λεωφορείο;
6. **Το αυτοκίνητο.** Είναι **πίσω** από το **σπίτι.**
7. Τέλεια, τα λέμε την **Πέμπτη**!

✤ In Greek, to express movement towards a place, use the accusative case, but for stating location or position, use the genitive or locative case.

1. Do you want to go **right** to the **apartment** for **coffee** on **Thursday**?
2. Yes, but I prefer **tea**. Is it **next to** the **station**?
3. No, it's **between** the **supermarket** and the **pharmacy**. **Here or there**?
4. **Here, inside the garden. It also has vegetables.**
5. Great, shall we take the **car** or the **bus**?
6. The **car**. It's **behind the house**.
7. Perfect, see you on **Thursday**!

✣ In Modern Greek culture, the first complete map of Greece was created by Rigas Feraios in 1797, aiming to inspire the Greek War of Independence.

1. Πάμε στο **εμπορικό κέντρο**;
2. Ναι, χρειάζομαι **τυρί** και **κοτόπουλο** από το **σούπερ μάρκετ**.
3. Πάρε ένα **καλάθι**. Πόσο είναι η **τιμή** του κοτόπουλου;
4. Έχει **έκπτωση**. Κοίτα την **απόδειξη**.
5. Ωραία! Πάμε στο **ταμείο**.
6. Μπορούμε να ζητήσουμε **επιστροφή χρημάτων** αν χρειαστεί;
7. Ναι, αλλά μόνο με την **απόδειξη**.

✤ In questions about shopping, the verb often comes before the subject, like "Πόσο κοστίζει αυτό;" (How much does this cost?).

DAY 44: SHOPPING III

1. Shall we go to the **shopping mall**?
2. Yes, I need **cheese** and **chicken** from the **supermarket**.
3. Grab a **basket**. How much is the **price** of the chicken?
4. It's on **discount**. Look at the **receipt**.
5. Great! Let's go to the **checkout**.
6. Can we ask for a **refund** if needed?
7. Yes, but only with the **receipt**.

♣ In Greece, it's customary to give an odd number of flowers as a gift, as even numbers are reserved for mourning.

ΗΜΈΡΑ ΝΟΎΜΕΡΟ 45: ΧΡΉΜΑΤΑ ΚΑΙ ΠΛΗΡΩΜΈΣ

1. Θέλω να **αγοράσω** ένα **αναψυκτικό** από το **σούπερ μάρκετ.**
2. Έχεις **μετρητά** ή θα πληρώσεις με **χρεωστική κάρτα**;
3. Μόνο **κέρματα** και ένα **χαρτονόμισμα** έχω. Πόσο κοστίζει;
4. Η **τιμή** είναι δύο ευρώ. Έχουμε και **έκπτωση** σήμερα.
5. Ωραία, θα πάρω δύο τότε. Πού είναι το **ταμείο**;
6. Εκεί, δίπλα στο **καλάθι**. Μπορείς να πληρώσεις και στον **Αυτόματο Τραπεζικό Μηχανισμό (ΑΤΜ)** αν θες.
7. Ευχαριστώ. Θα χρησιμοποιήσω τα **μετρητά**. Μπορώ να έχω μια **απόδειξη**;
8. Φυσικά, να η **απόδειξή** σου και η **επιστροφή χρημάτων**.
9. Ευχαριστώ πολύ!

✤ In Greek, the object (money amount) usually comes after the verb in sentences about payments, for example, "Πληρώνω δέκα ευρώ." (I pay ten euros).

1. I want to **buy** a **soda from the supermarket**.
2. Do you have **cash** or will you pay with a **debit card**?
3. I only have **coins** and a **banknote**. How much does it cost?
4. The **price** is two euros. We also have a **discount** today.
5. Great, I'll take two then. Where is the **cashier**?
6. There, next to the **basket**. You can also pay at the **Automated Teller Machine (ATM)** if you want.
7. Thank you. I'll use the **cash**. Can I have a **receipt**?
8. Of course, here's your **receipt** and your **change**.
9. Thank you very much!

✤ In Greece, the world's oldest known analog computer, the Antikythera mechanism, was used to predict astronomical positions and eclipses for calendrical and astrological purposes, as well as the Olympiads, the cycles of the ancient Olympic Games, showcasing an early intersection of technology, economy, and culture.

ΗΜΈΡΑ ΝΟΎΜΕΡΟ 46: ΚΑΙΡΌΣ ΚΑΙ ΦΎΣΗ 🌱

1. Έχεις δει την **πρόγνωση** του **καιρού** για αύριο;
2. Ναι, λέει ότι θα είναι **υγρό** με **ψιλόβροχο** το πρωί.
3. Και το απόγευμα;
4. Θα έχουμε **ηλιοφάνεια** αλλά με κάποια **σύννεφα**.
5. Α, καλά νέα! Μήπως είδες αν θα έχουμε **κεραυνούς** και **αστραπές**;
6. Όχι, δεν είπαν για **κεραυνούς**. Μόνο λίγο **ψιλόβροχο**.
7. Ελπίζω να δούμε και **ουράνιο τόξο** μετά τη βροχή.
8. Ναι, θα ήταν όμορφο. Και χωρίς **νιφάδες χιονιού** είναι ακόμα καλύτερα.
9. Συμφωνώ. Ας ελπίσουμε σε έναν όμορφο **καιρό**!

✤ In Greek, to describe the weather, we often use impersonal expressions that start with "Είναι" (It is) followed by an adjective, like "Είναι ζεστό" (It is hot).

DAY 46: WEATHER AND NATURE

1. Have you seen the **weather forecast** for tomorrow?
2. Yes, it says it will be **humid** with **light rain** in the morning.
3. And in the afternoon?
4. We will have **sunshine** but with some **clouds**.
5. Ah, good news! Did you see if we will have **thunder** and **lightning**?
6. No, they didn't mention **thunder**. Just a little **light rain**.
7. I hope we see a **rainbow** after the rain.
8. Yes, that would be beautiful. And without **snowflakes** it's even better.
9. I agree. Let's hope for beautiful **weather**!

✤ In Modern Greek culture, it's believed that the winds are the quarreling spirits of ancient gods, still trying to assert their power over the land and sea.

1. Έχεις δει την **πρόγνωση** για αύριο;
2. Ναι, λένε ότι θα έχουμε **θύελλα**.
3. Πραγματικά; Πρέπει να πάω στο **σούπερ μάρκετ** να αγοράσω πράγματα.
4. Καλή ιδέα. Μην ξεχάσεις να πάρεις μια **απόδειξη** για τις αγορές σου.
5. Θα προσέξω. Ελπίζω οι **εκπτώσεις** να είναι καλές.
6. Μετά την **θύελλα**, θέλεις να πάμε στην **παραλία**;
7. Μόνο αν είναι **ήρεμος** ο καιρός. Δεν θέλω άλλες **καταστροφές**.
8. Συμφωνώ. Ας ελπίσουμε για έναν **ήρεμο** καιρό.

✤ In Greek, the pronunciation of "γ" changes to a soft "y" sound before "ε" or "ι", making words related to disasters and geography like "γεωγραφία" sound like "yeografía".

DAY 47: DISASTERS AND GEOGRAPHY 🌱

1. Have you seen the **forecast** for tomorrow?
2. Yes, they say we're going to have a **storm**.
3. Really? I need to go to the **supermarket** to buy some things.
4. Good idea. Don't forget to get a **receipt** for your purchases.
5. I'll be careful. I hope the **discounts** are good.
6. After the **storm**, do you want to go to the **beach**?
7. Only if the weather is **calm**. I don't want any more **disasters**.
8. I agree. Let's hope for **calm** weather.

❖ In Greek folklore, earthquakes are said to be caused by the god Poseidon striking the earth with his trident.

1. Τι είναι το αγαπημένο σου **χρώμα**;
2. Μου αρέσει πολύ το **μπλε**.
3. Εγώ προτιμώ το **πράσινο**. Είναι τόσο ήρεμο.
4. Και το **κίτρινο**; Σου αρέσει;
5. Ναι, είναι χαρούμενο **χρώμα**. Αλλά δεν είναι σαν το **μαύρο**.
6. Το **μαύρο** είναι κλασικό. Αλλά το **λευκό** είναι πιο φωτεινό.
7. Συμφωνώ. Και το **ροζ**;
8. Το **ροζ** είναι όμορφο, αλλά προτιμώ το **καφέ**.
9. Και το **γκρι**; Είναι καλό για συνδυασμούς.
10. Ναι, αλλά το **χρυσό** είναι το αγαπημένο μου για διακόσμηση.

✤ In Greek, the gender of a color adjective must match the gender of the noun it describes.

1. What's your favorite **color?**
2. I really like **blue.**
3. I prefer **green.** It's so calming.
4. And **yellow?** Do you like it?
5. Yes, it's a happy **color.** But it's not like **black.**
6. **Black is classic. But white** is brighter.
7. I agree. And **pink?**
8. **Pink is beautiful, but I prefer brown.**
9. And **gray?** It's good for combinations.
10. Yes, but **gold** is my favorite for decoration.

✤ In Greece, the Color Day Festival is a vibrant event where thousands gather to throw colored powders, celebrating music and life in an explosion of hues.

1. Έχεις **Wi-Fi**;
2. Ναι, θέλεις τον κωδικό;
3. Θα ήθελα, ευχαριστώ. Θέλω να τσεκάρω τα **κοινωνικά δίκτυα** στο **έξυπνο κινητό** μου.
4. Φυσικά. Επίσης, μπορείς να χρησιμοποιήσεις τον **υπολογιστή** μου αν θες.
5. Προτιμώ το **φορητό υπολογιστή** μου. Έχω μια σημαντική **εφαρμογή** που πρέπει να χρησιμοποιήσω.
6. Καταλαβαίνω. Θέλεις να σου **κατεβάσω** κάτι;
7. Όχι, ευχαριστώ. Απλά θα στείλω ένα **ηλεκτρονικό ταχυδρομείο** και θα χρησιμοποιήσω τον **περιηγητή**.

✿ In Modern Greek, the stress mark (accent) moves to the antepenultimate syllable when forming the plural of most technology-related nouns ending in -ος.

1. Do you have **Wi-Fi**?
2. Yes, do you want the password?
3. I would, thank you. I want to check my **social networks** on my **smartphone**.
4. Of course. Also, you can use my **computer** if you want.
5. I prefer my **laptop**. I have an important **application** I need to use.
6. I understand. Do you want me to **download** anything for you?
7. No, thank you. I'll just send an **email** and use the **browser**.

❖ In Greece, the world's first commercial digital terrestrial television platform, Nova, was launched in 1999, revolutionizing the way Greeks watch TV.

1. Έχεις δει τις **ειδήσεις** στην **τηλεόραση** σήμερα;
2. Όχι, έχασα το **κανάλι.** Τι έγινε;
3. Υπήρξε μεγάλος **σεισμός** στην Ιαπωνία. Προσπαθώ να βρω περισσότερες πληροφορίες στο **ίντερνετ.**
4. Χρησιμοποιείς τον **υπολογιστή** ή το **έξυπνο κινητό**;
5. Το **έξυπνο κινητό.** Είναι πιο βολικό. Αλλά ξέχασα τον **κωδικό πρόσβασης** για το **ηλεκτρονικό ταχυδρομείο.**
6. Μπορείς να αλλάξεις τον κωδικό. Έχεις το **όνομα χρήστη**;
7. Ναι, το έχω. Θα το κάνω αμέσως. Ευχαριστώ!

✤ In Greek, words with more than one syllable always have a written accent to show where the stress falls, such as in "τεχνολογία" (technology), where the accent is on the second-to-last syllable.

1. Have you seen the **news** on **TV** today?
2. No, I missed the **channel**. What happened?
3. There was a big **earthquake** in Japan. I'm trying to find more information on the **internet**.
4. Are you using the **computer** or the **smartphone**?
5. The **smartphone**. It's more convenient. But I forgot the **password** for my **email**.
6. You can change the password. Do you have the **username**?
7. Yes, I have it. I'll do it right away. Thank you!

✤ In Greece, Facebook played a pivotal role in organizing the "Aganaktismenoi" (Indignant Citizens Movement) protests in Syntagma Square in 2011, showcasing the power of social media in mobilizing citizens for political action.

CHALLENGE NO. 5

LISTEN TO A PODCAST IN MODERN GREEK AND SUMMARIZE IT, IN WRITING OR ORALLY.

"Η περιέργεια μας οδηγεί σε νέους δρόμους."

"Curiosity leads us to new paths."

1. Μου αρέσει το **πουλί** στον κήπο.
2. Και εμένα. Αλλά προτιμώ τη **γάτα**.
3. Έχεις δει το **άλογο** στο χωράφι;
4. Ναι, είναι όμορφο. Και ο **σκύλος** είναι φιλικός.
5. Τα **ψάρια** στη λίμνη είναι χρωματιστά.
6. Στην αυλή έχουμε **κοτόπουλο** και **αγελάδα**.
7. Το **χοιρινό** δεν είναι ζώο εδώ.
8. Α, και μην ξεχάσουμε το **ποντίκι** στο σπίτι!
9. Ναι, πρέπει να προσέχουμε τα τρόφιμα.

✤ In Greek, to link a noun (like an animal) with an adjective, we use the verb "είναι" (to be),

as in "Ο σκύλος είναι μεγάλος" (The dog is big).

1. I like the **bird** in the garden.
2. Me too. But I prefer the **cat**.
3. Have you seen the **horse** in the field?
4. Yes, it's beautiful. And the **dog** is friendly.
5. The **fish** in the lake are colorful.
6. In the yard, we have a **chicken** and a **cow**.
7. The **pork** is not an animal here.
8. Oh, and let's not forget the **mouse** in the house!
9. Yes, we need to be careful with the food.

✤ In Modern Greek culture, the phoenix symbolizes rebirth and renewal, often associated with the nation's resilience and revival through its history.

1. Μου αρέσει να περπατώ στο **δάσος** και να βλέπω τα **δέντρα**.
2. Και εμένα! Τα **φυτά** και τα **λουλούδια** με κάνουν πολύ **χαρούμενη**.
3. Έχεις δει τη **ζούγκλα** στο **βουνό**; Είναι γεμάτη **φύλλα** και **χόρτο**.
4. Όχι, αλλά θα ήθελα. Λένε ότι εκεί ζουν πολλά **ζώα**.
5. Ναι, και τα **πουλιά** είναι πανέμορφα. Αγαπώ επίσης τον **ωκεανό** και τα **ποτάμια**.
6. Το νερό φέρνει ζωή στα **φυτά**. Είμαι πάντα **χαλαρή** όταν είμαι κοντά στη φύση.

✤ In Greek, when a word ending in a vowel is followed by another word beginning with a vowel, we often drop the final vowel of the first word, like in "τ' άνθη" (the flowers) instead of "τα άνθη".

1. I like to walk in the **forest** and see the **trees**.
2. Me too! The **plants** and **flowers** make me very **happy**.
3. Have you seen the **jungle** on the **mountain**? It's full of **leaves** and **grass**.
4. No, but I would like to. They say many **animals** live there.
5. Yes, and the **birds** are beautiful. I also love the **ocean** and the **rivers**.
6. Water brings life to the **plants**. I'm always **relaxed** when I'm close to nature.

✤ In Modern Greece, the ancient practice of using dittany of Crete, a plant endemic to the island, persists for its remarkable healing properties, famously believed to have saved the life of Aristotle.

1. Έχεις δει το **φυτό** μου; Είναι **τριάντα ένα** εκατοστά ψηλό.
2. Όχι, αλλά είδα ένα **δέντρο τριάντα δύο** εκατοστά. Είναι δικό σου;
3. Όχι, το δικό μου έχει **λουλούδια** και **φύλλα**. Ίσως είναι **τριάντα τρία** εκατοστά τώρα.
4. Α, βρήκα ένα **χόρτο τριάντα τέσσερα εκατοστά δίπλα στην τηλεόραση**.
5. Αυτό είναι! Πάνω ή κάτω από το **κανάλι** με τις **ειδήσεις**;
6. **Δεξιά από το ραδιόφωνο, κοντά στο τηλεχειριστήριο**.
7. Αισθάνομαι λίγο **ανήσυχος**. Μήπως το πότισες;
8. Ναι, μην είσαι **φοβισμένος**. Το φροντίζω καλά.
9. Ευχαριστώ! Τώρα είμαι λιγότερο **αγχωμένος**.

❖ In Greek, when counting from 31 to 39, the word for "and" (και) contracts with the tens (τριάντα) to form a single word, like "τριάντα" (30) becomes "τριανταένα" for 31.

DAY 53: NUMBERS 31-40 🌱

1. Have you seen my **plant**? It's **thirty-one** centimeters tall.

2. No, but I saw a **tree thirty-two** centimeters tall. Is it yours?

3. No, mine has **flowers** and **leaves**. Maybe it's **thirty-three** centimeters now.

4. Ah, I found a **weed thirty-four centimeters tall next to the television**.

5. That's it! Above or below the **news channel**?

6. **Right from the radio, near the remote control**.

7. I feel a bit **anxious**. Did you water it?

8. Yes, don't be **scared**. I take good care of it.

9. Thank you! Now I'm less **stressed**.

✤ In Greece, houses traditionally have blue doors because it's believed the color wards off evil spirits, combining aesthetic appeal with cultural numerology.

ΗΜΈΡΑ ΝΟΎΜΕΡΟ 54: ΜΟΥΣΙΚΉ ΚΑΙ ΔΙΑΣΚΈΔΑΣΗ

1. Θέλεις να πάμε σε μια **συναυλία** απόψε;
2. Ποιο **συγκρότημα** παίζει;
3. Ένας πολύ καλός **τραγουδιστής**. Θα ακούσουμε ωραία **τραγούδια**.
4. Ωραία! Μου αρέσει πολύ η **μουσική** και ο **χορός**.
5. Μετά, θέλεις να πάμε στο **θέατρο** ή να δούμε μια **ταινία**;
6. Προτιμώ **ταινία**. Και μετά, μπορούμε να ακούσουμε **ραδιόφωνο** στο αυτοκίνητο.
7. Τέλεια! Θα είναι μια υπέροχη βραδιά με πολλή **διασκέδαση**.

❖ In Greek, the determiner changes form to match the gender, number, and case of the noun it describes, so for "the song" we say "το τραγούδι" and for "the songs" we say "τα τραγούδια".

1. Do you want to go to a **concert** tonight?
2. Which **band** is playing?
3. A very good **singer**. We'll hear some nice **songs**.
4. Great! I really like **music** and **dancing**.
5. Afterwards, do you want to go to the **theater** or watch a **movie**?
6. I prefer a **movie**. And then, we can listen to the **radio** in the car.
7. Perfect! It's going to be a wonderful evening with lots of **fun**.

✤ The bouzouki, a central instrument in Greek music, originally had only three strings, symbolizing the three Greek seas: the Aegean, the Ionian, and the Mediterranean.

1. Θέλεις να πάμε στο **αεροδρόμιο** με **αυτοκίνητο** ή με **ταξί**;
2. Προτιμώ με **ταξί**. Είναι πιο άνετο.
3. Και μετά το **αεροπλάνο**, θα πάρουμε **τρένο** ή **λεωφορείο για το λιμάνι**;
4. Νομίζω το **τρένο** είναι καλύτερη επιλογή. Είναι πιο γρήγορο.
5. Στο **λιμάνι**, θα πάρουμε **πλοίο** για το νησί;
6. Ναι, το **πλοίο** είναι η μόνη επιλογή. Έχεις πάρει **μετρητά** ή **χρεωστική κάρτα**;
7. Έχω και τα δύο. Και μην ξεχνάς το **ποδήλατο** για εκεί.
8. Α, ναι! Θα είναι ωραίο να εξερευνήσουμε με **ποδήλατο**.

✤ In Greek, to express "some" or "any" when talking about means of transportation, use "κάποιος, κάποια, κάποιο" before the noun, matching the noun's gender.

DAY 55: TRAVEL AND TRANSPORTATION III

1. Do you want to go to the **airport** by **car** or by **taxi**?
2. I prefer by **taxi**. It's more comfortable.
3. And after the **plane**, shall we take a **train** or **bus** to the **port**?
4. I think the **train** is a better choice. It's faster.
5. At the **port**, will we take a **ship** to the island?
6. Yes, the **ship** is the only option. Have you taken **cash** or a **debit card**?
7. I have both. And don't forget the **bicycle** for there.
8. Ah, yes! It will be nice to explore by **bicycle**.

✤ In modern Greece, the tradition of naming ships after ancient heroes and myths continues, symbolizing the pioneering spirit of exploration and adventure that spans millennia.

1. Πάμε στο **εμπορικό κέντρο**;
2. Ναι, χρειάζομαι **ρούχα** και **μπουφάν**.
3. Θέλω να δω και τα **κοσμήματα**. Έχω ακούσει για **κολιέ** και **σκουλαρίκια** με **έκπτωση**.
4. Α, καλή ιδέα! Μετά, πάμε **σούπερ μάρκετ** ή **μπακάλικο**;
5. **Σούπερ μάρκετ**. Έχουμε περισσότερες επιλογές εκεί.
6. Ελπίζω να βρούμε καλές **εκπτώσεις**.

✤ In Modern Greek, to show possession, you add the possessive pronoun before the noun, like in "Το βιβλίο μου" (My book).

1. Shall we go to the **shopping mall**?
2. Yes, I need **clothes** and a **jacket**.
3. I want to check out the **jewelry** too. I've heard about **necklaces** and **earrings** on **sale**.
4. Oh, good idea! Afterwards, shall we go to a **supermarket** or a **grocery store**?
5. **Supermarket**. We have more options there.
6. I hope we find good **discounts**.

❖ In Athens, the Monastiraki flea market comes alive every Sunday, turning the neighborhood into a treasure trove of vintage finds and local artifacts.

1. Έχεις πονοκέφαλο;
2. Ναι, και πονάει και το **αυτί** μου.
3. Ίσως να έχεις κρύωση. Πρέπει να πιεις ένα **τσάι**.
4. Καλή ιδέα. Εσύ πώς αισθάνεσαι;
5. Εγώ είμαι καλά, αλλά χθες είχα πόνο στο **πόδι**.
6. Πώς συνέβη αυτό;
7. Έπεσα όταν έτρεχα λόγω της **θύελλας**.
8. Ωχ! Πρέπει να προσέχουμε περισσότερο. Θα πας στον γιατρό;
9. Όχι, τώρα είναι καλύτερα. Ας πάμε για **καφέ** αντί για αυτό.

✤ In Greek, to point out something related to body and health, use "αυτός" (this) for masculine, "αυτή" (this) for feminine, and "αυτό" (this) for neuter nouns.

1. Do you have a headache?
2. Yes, and my **ear** hurts too.
3. You might have a cold. You should drink some **tea**.
4. Good idea. How are you feeling?
5. I'm fine, but yesterday I had a pain in my **leg**.
6. How did that happen?
7. I fell while running because of the **storm**.
8. Oh! We need to be more careful. Are you going to see a doctor?
9. No, it's better now. Let's go for **coffee** instead.

✤ In Modern Greece, the practice of "xematiasma" or "the evil eye" is still widely believed, where symptoms of fatigue or headache are often cured through a ritual involving prayers and the sign of the cross.

1. Θέλω να γίνω **γιατρός**.
2. Γιατί;
3. Μου αρέσει να βοηθάω τους ανθρώπους.
   Και εσύ;
4. Εγώ θέλω να είμαι **σεφ**.
5. Πολύ ενδιαφέρον! Τι θα μαγειρέψεις;
6. Κοτόπουλο με **πιπέρι** και **τυρί**.
7. Ακούγεται νόστιμο! Ο αδερφός μου είναι **δικηγόρος**.
8. Και η αδερφή μου είναι **δασκάλα**.
9. Ωραία επαγγέλματα!

✤ In Greek, to describe someone's profession, you use the relative pronoun "που" (who/that) after the profession to add information about the job, like "Είναι ο γιατρός που εργάζεται στο νοσοκομείο" (He is the doctor who works at the hospital).

1. I want to become a **doctor**.
2. Why?
3. I like helping people. And you?
4. I want to be a **chef**.
5. Very interesting! What will you cook?
6. Chicken with **pepper** and **cheese**.
7. Sounds delicious! My brother is a **lawyer**.
8. And my sister is a **teacher**.
9. Nice professions!

♣ In Modern Greece, the art of worry bead crafting, known as "komboloi," has evolved from a simple pastime into a symbol of cultural identity and stress relief.

1. Έχεις **καναπέ** στο σαλόνι σου;
2. Ναι, και δίπλα έχω ένα **τραπέζι** με μία **λάμπα** πάνω.
3. Ωραία! Και τι έχεις στην κουζίνα;
4. Έναν **φούρνο**, ένα **ψυγείο** και πολλές **καρέκλες** γύρω από το **τραπέζι**.
5. Και το **κρεβάτι** σου; Πού είναι;
6. Στο δωμάτιο με το μεγάλο **παράθυρο** και δίπλα στη **πόρτα**.
7. Έχεις και **ρολόι**;
8. Ναι, πάνω από το **κρεβάτι**.

✤ In Greek, to say "a" or "an" for indefinite household items, use "ένας" for masculine nouns, "μία" for feminine nouns, and "ένα" for neuter nouns before the item's name.

1. Do you have a **sofa** in your living room?
2. Yes, and next to it, I have a **table** with a **lamp** on it.
3. Nice! And what do you have in the kitchen?
4. An **oven**, a **refrigerator**, and many **chairs** around the **table**.
5. And your **bed**? Where is it?
6. In the room with the big **window** and next to the **door**.
7. Do you also have a **clock**?
8. Yes, above the **bed**.

✤ In Greece, the sea sponge divers of Kalymnos are renowned for pioneering diving techniques to harvest natural sponges, a practice dating back to ancient times.

ΗΜΈΡΑ ΝΟΎΜΕΡΟ 60: ΜΈΤΡΑ ΚΑΙ ΜΈΓΕΘΟΣ

1. Πόσο **μήκος** έχει ο καναπές;
2. Έχει δύο **μέτρα** και το **πλάτος** του είναι ενάμισι **μέτρο**.
3. Και το **ψυγείο**; Πόσο **ύψος** έχει;
4. Το **ψυγείο** έχει ένα **μέτρο** και ογδόντα **εκατοστά** **ύψος**.
5. Το **βάρος** του **φούρνου** πόσα **κιλά** είναι;
6. Είναι σαράντα **κιλά**. Και το **σχήμα** του **πάτου**;
7. Είναι κυκλικό. Και το **μέγεθος** της **λάμπας**;
8. Είναι πενήντα **εκατοστά** σε **ύψος**.

✤ In Modern Greek, to form the present participle for expressing measurements and size, add "-οντας" to the verb stem, like "μετρώντας" (measuring).

1. How long is the couch?
2. It is two **meters** long and its **width** is one and a half **meters**.
3. And the **refrigerator**? How tall is it?
4. The **refrigerator** is one **meter** and eighty **centimeters** tall.
5. How much does the **oven weigh**?
6. It weighs forty **kilos**. And the **shape** of the **plate**?
7. It is round. And the **size** of the **lamp**?
8. It is fifty **centimeters** tall.

❖ Modern Greeks still use the ancient term "stremma" to measure land, equivalent to 1,000 square meters.

CHALLENGE NO. 6

RECORD A SHORT AUDIO WHERE YOU TALK ABOUT YOUR PROGRESS IN MODERN GREEK.

"Η διαφορετικότητα εμπλουτίζει την ανθρώπινη εμπειρία."

"Diversity enriches the human experience."

ΗΜΈΡΑ ΑΡΙΘ. 61: ΤΡΟΦΉ ΚΑΙ ΔΙΑΤΡΟΦΉ ΙΙ

1. Θέλεις **ζυμαρικά** με **βούτυρο** και **πιπέρι**;
2. Όχι, προτιμώ **κοτόπουλο** με **ρύζι**.
3. Έχουμε επίσης **μοσχάρι** ή **χοιρινό**.
4. Μήπως έχετε κάτι ελαφρύ; Ίσως **ψωμί** και **τυρί**;
5. Βεβαίως, και για επιδόρπιο;
6. Έχετε **παγωτό**;
7. Ναι, έχουμε πολλές γεύσεις.
8. Τέλεια, θα πάρω αυτό.

✤ In Greek, to form the past participle for regular verbs, add "μένος, μένη, μένο" to the verb stem, which is used to describe a completed action related to food, like "τηγανισμένος πατάτες" for "fried potatoes."

1. Do you want **pasta** with **butter** and **pepper**?
2. No, I prefer **chicken** with **rice**.
3. We also have **beef** or **pork**.
4. Could I have something light? Maybe **bread** and **cheese**?
5. Certainly, and for dessert?
6. Do you have **ice cream**?
7. Yes, we have many flavors.
8. Perfect, I'll have that.

✤ In Modern Greek culture, the tradition of "philoxenia" - or love of strangers - has evolved to include sharing innovative fusion dishes that blend ancient recipes with contemporary flavors.

ΗΜΈΡΑ ΝΟΎΜΕΡΟ 62: ΗΜΈΡΕΣ ΤΗΣ ΕΒΔΟΜΆΔΑΣ

1. Τι κάνουμε **Σάββατο**;
2. Θέλεις να μαγειρέψουμε **ζυμαρικά**;
3. Ναι, με **βούτυρο** και **πιπέρι**;
4. Ακριβώς. Και την **Κυριακή**;
5. Ίσως κάτι με **κοτόπουλο**. Θα το βάλουμε στον **φούρνο**.
6. Καλή ιδέα. Και το **σαββατοκύριακο** θα φυτέψουμε **λουλούδια** στον κήπο;
7. Ναι, και θα ποτίσουμε τα **φυτά**.
8. Αν χρειαστούμε **βοήθεια**, θα καλέσουμε τον γείτονα;
9. Φυσικά, αλλά ελπίζω να μην χρειαστεί να καλέσουμε **γιατρό**!

✤ In Modern Greek, the gerund does not exist; instead, we use the present participle or other verb forms to describe ongoing actions related to days of the week.

174

1. What are we doing **Saturday**?
2. Do you want to cook **pasta**?
3. Yes, with **butter** and **pepper**?
4. Exactly. And on **Sunday**?
5. Maybe something with **chicken**. We'll put it in the **oven**.
6. Good idea. And over the **weekend**, shall we plant **flowers** in the garden?
7. Yes, and we'll water the **plants**.
8. If we need **help**, shall we call the neighbor?
9. Of course, but I hope we won't need to call a **doctor**!

✤ In Modern Greek culture, many people consult astrologers to pick auspicious days for weddings, believing the alignment of stars can bless the union.

1. **Σήμερα** είναι **Χειμώνας**. Εσύ τι κάνεις **απόγευμα**;
2. Μένω σπίτι και διαβάζω. Και εσύ;
3. Εγώ προτιμώ να περπατώ το **πρωί**. Είναι πιο ζεστό.
4. Αύριο θα είναι **Άνοιξη**;
5. Όχι, ακόμα είναι **Χειμώνας**. Αλλά **αύριο** θα είναι πιο ζεστό.
6. Καλά, ίσως βγω για λίγο το **βράδυ**.
7. Ναι, το **βράδυ** είναι ωραία. Ελπίζω να μην κάνει πολύ κρύο.
8. Εγώ ελπίζω το **καλοκαίρι** να έρθει γρήγορα.
9. Κι εγώ. Μου αρέσει περισσότερο η ζέστη.

✤ In Modern Greek, the infinitive form is not used; instead, we use the subjunctive mood with "να" to express actions related to weather and seasons, like "Να βρέξει" (to rain).

1. **Today** is **Winter**. What are you doing **in the afternoon**?
2. I stay home and read. And you?
3. I prefer to walk **in the morning**. It's warmer.
4. Will it be **Spring** tomorrow?
5. No, it's still **Winter**. But **tomorrow** will be warmer.
6. Okay, maybe I'll go out for a bit **in the evening**.
7. Yes, **the evening** is nice. I hope it's not too cold.
8. I hope **summer** comes quickly.
9. Me too. I like the warmth more.

✤ In Modern Greek music, the season of summer is often celebrated with vibrant island melodies that evoke the country's picturesque landscapes and lively festivals.

1. **Θεία**, τι θα κάνουμε **σήμερα**;
2. Θα πάμε σε μια **συναυλία**, **ανιψιέ** μου.
3. Ποιο **συγκρότημα** θα δούμε;
4. Ένα που αρέσει και στον **ξάδερφο** σου. Θα έρθει και ο **σύντροφος** της **θείας**.
5. Και μετά τη **συναυλία**;
6. Θα φάμε **ζυμαρικά** με **βούτυρο** και **πιπέρι**, **ανιψιέ** μου.
7. Ωραία! Θα είναι εκεί και η **εγγονή** σου;
8. Ναι, και ο **εγγονός**. Θα είναι μια όμορφη **ημέρα**.

✤ In Greek, many family-related words share a common root, so by changing the ending, you can change the word from "brother" (αδελφός) to "sister" (αδελφή).

DAY 64: FAMILY II

1. **Aunt**, what are we going to do **today**?
2. We're going to a **concert, my nephew**.
3. Which **band** are we going to see?
4. One that your **cousin** likes too. Your **aunt's partner** will also come.
5. And after the **concert**?
6. We'll eat **pasta** with **butter** and **pepper, my nephew**.
7. Great! Will your **granddaughter** be there too?
8. Yes, and the **grandson**. It's going to be a beautiful **day**.

✤ In Modern Greek families, it's common to name children after their grandparents, weaving a tale of heritage and continuity through generations.

ΗΜΈΡΑ ΝΟΎΜΕΡΟ 65: ΚΑΤΕΥΘΎΝΣΕΙΣ ΚΑΙ ΤΟΠΟΘΕΣΊΕΣ ΙΙΙ 🌱

1. **Πάνω** στον **καναπέ**, πού είναι το **αυτοκίνητο**;
2. **Κάτω από το τραπέζι**. Πάμε ευθεία στο αεροδρόμιο;
3. Όχι, **στρίψε αριστερά και μετά δεξιά**. Είναι **κοντά ή μακριά**;
4. Είναι **κοντά**, **ανάμεσα στο σπίτι και το πάρκο**.
5. Καλά, **σταμάτα** εδώ. Πόσο **μακριά** είναι το **λεωφορείο**;
6. Πολύ **κοντά**, **πάνω** στη γωνία.

✤ In Greek, verbs change form to match the subject and indicate direction or location, such as "πηγαίνω" (I go) becoming "πηγαίνεις" (you go).

1. **On** the **couch,** where is the **car?**
2. **Under the table. Shall we go straight to the airport?**
3. No, **turn left and then right. Is it close or far?**
4. It's **close, between the house and the park.**
5. Okay, **stop** here. How **far** is the **bus?**
6. Very **close, on** the corner.

❖ In Modern Greek literature, Nikos Kazantzakis' "Zorba the Greek" embarks on a journey of self-discovery and freedom, reflecting Greece's quest for identity amidst tradition and modernity.

1. **Είμαι τόσο ενθουσιασμένος!** Αγόρασα ένα νέο μπουφάν από το εμπορικό κέντρο.
2. Αλήθεια; Εγώ είμαι λίγο **νευρικός**. Δεν ξέρω αν πρέπει να πάω σήμερα ή αύριο.
3. Μην είσαι **αγχωμένος**. Πάμε μαζί αύριο το πρωί; Θα είμαι **χαρούμενος** να σε βοηθήσω.
4. Αυτό θα ήταν ωραίο. Είμαι πάντα **ανήσυχος** όταν πρέπει να κάνω αγορές μόνος.
5. Κανένα πρόβλημα! Θα είμαι **περήφανος** να σε βοηθήσω να βρεις ό,τι χρειάζεσαι.
6. Ευχαριστώ πολύ. Τώρα αισθάνομαι πιο **χαλαρός**.

❖ In Modern Greek, to express emotions in compound tenses, we often use the verb "έχω" (to have) followed by the main verb in its participle form.

1. **I'm so excited**! I bought a new jacket from the mall.
2. Really? I'm a bit **nervous**. I don't know if I should go today or tomorrow.
3. Don't be **stressed**. Shall we go together tomorrow morning? I'd be **happy** to help you.
4. That would be nice. I'm always **anxious** when I have to shop alone.
5. No problem! I'll be **proud** to help you find whatever you need.
6. Thank you so much. Now I feel more **relaxed**.

✤ In Modern Greek art, the color blue is often used to evoke a sense of calm and serenity, reflecting Greece's deep connection with the sea and sky.

ΗΜΈΡΑ ΝΟΎΜΕΡΟ 67: ΤΕΧΝΟΛΟΓΊΑ ΚΑΙ ΜΈΣΑ ΕΝΗΜΈΡΩΣΗΣ 🌱

1. Έχεις **Ίντερνετ** στο **έξυπνο κινητό** σου;
2. Ναι, χρησιμοποιώ **Wi-Fi**. Και εσύ;
3. Εγώ βλέπω **ιστοσελίδες** και στέλνω **ηλεκτρονικά ταχυδρομεία σε απευθείας σύνδεση**.
4. Έχεις αγαπημένη **εφαρμογή**;
5. Ναι, μου αρέσουν τα **κοινωνικά δίκτυα** και να διαβάζω **ιστολόγια**.
6. Πώς βρίσκεις τις **ιστοσελίδες**;
7. Με τον **περιηγητή** στο κινητό. Είναι πολύ εύκολο.

❖ In Modern Greek, to express the infinitive mood when talking about technology and media, we often use the structure "να + verb" as in "Θέλω να παρακολουθήσω μια ταινία" (I want to watch a movie).

1. Do you have **Internet** on your **smartphone**?
2. Yes, I use **Wi-Fi**. What about you?
3. I browse **websites** and send **emails online**.
4. Do you have a favorite **app**?
5. Yes, I like **social networks** and reading **blogs**.
6. How do you find the **websites**?
7. With the **browser** on my phone. It's very easy.

❖ In Greece, the newspaper "Eleftherotypia" was founded in 1975, symbolizing freedom of press after the fall of the military junta.

1. Θέλεις να πάμε στη **διάλεξη** για **ζωγραφική** σήμερα;
2. Ναι, αλλά πρέπει να βρω ένα **βιβλίο** για την **ποίηση** πρώτα.
3. Στο **μπακάλικο** ή στο **εμπορικό κέντρο**; Έχουν **έκπτωση** στα **βιβλία**.
4. Στο **εμπορικό κέντρο**. Θέλω να δω και **φωτογραφίες**.
5. Καλή ιδέα. Μετά, μπορούμε να πάμε για καφέ.
6. Ναι, και να συζητήσουμε για το **μυθιστόρημα** που διαβάζω.
7. Α, **μυθοπλασία** ή **μη-μυθοπλασία**;
8. **Μυθοπλασία**. Είναι πολύ ενδιαφέρον.

✤ In Modern Greek, the participle mode is used to describe an action related to the main verb, like in reading a book while enjoying the sun.

1. Do you want to go to the **lecture** on **painting** today?
2. Yes, but I need to find a **book** on **poetry** first.
3. At the **grocery store** or the **shopping mall**? They have a **discount** on **books**.
4. At the **shopping mall**. I also want to look at some **photographs**.
5. Good idea. Afterward, we can go for coffee.
6. Yes, and discuss the **novel** I'm reading.
7. Oh, **fiction** or **non-fiction**?
8. **Fiction**. It's very interesting.

✤ The Benaki Museum in Athens houses a diverse collection spanning Greece's history, from ancient to modern times, in a beautiful neoclassical building.

1. Θέλω να πάω στο **αεροδρόμιο**. Πόσο κοστίζει το **ταξί**;
2. Έχεις **χρεωστική κάρτα** ή **μετρητά**;
3. Έχω και τα δύο. Και **βαλίτσα** και **σακίδιο πλάτης**.
4. Το **ταξί** κοστίζει 20 ευρώ. Είσαι **ενθουσιασμένος** για το ταξίδι;
5. Ναι, πολύ! Θα μείνω σε ένα **ξενοδοχείο** κοντά στον **σιδηροδρομικό σταθμό**.
6. Ωραία! Έχεις επισκεφθεί την **πρεσβεία** για πληροφορίες;
7. Όχι ακόμα. Πρέπει να πάω;
8. Ναι, είναι καλή ιδέα. Καλό ταξίδι και να είσαι **χαρούμενος**!

✤ In Modern Greek, to express an action related to travel or places in the gerund mode, we often use the verb in its present participle form, adding -οντας or -ώντας to the stem, like "ταξιδεύοντας" (traveling).

1. I want to go to the **airport**. How much does the **taxi** cost?
2. Do you have a **debit card** or **cash**?
3. I have both. And a **suitcase** and a **backpack**.
4. The **taxi** costs 20 euros. Are you **excited** about the trip?
5. Yes, very! I will stay at a **hotel** near the **train station**.
6. Nice! Have you visited the **embassy** for information?
7. Not yet. Should I go?
8. Yes, it's a good idea. Have a good trip and be **happy**!

❖ In Greece, the breathtaking Meteora monasteries are perched atop towering rock formations, originally accessible only by ladders and ropes, symbolizing a closer connection to the divine.

1. Πόσες βαλίτσες έχεις;
2. **Δεκαέξι.**
3. Και πόσα κιλά είναι;
4. **Δεκαοκτώ** κιλά.
5. Θα πάμε με ταξί στο αεροδρόμιο;
6. Όχι, προτιμώ το σιδηροδρομικό σταθμό. Είναι πιο άνετο.
7. Έχεις κλείσει ξενοδοχείο;
8. Ναι, μέσω μιας ιστοσελίδας. Βρήκα ένα χόστελ για **δεκαεπτά** νύχτες.
9. Και η πρόγνωση του καιρού;
10. Λέει ότι θα είναι υγρός καιρός με αστραπές.

✤ In Modern Greek, when counting from 11 to 20, the number changes form based on whether it's used with a masculine, feminine, or neuter noun, reflecting the noun's grammatical gender.

1. How many suitcases do you have?
2. **Sixteen**.
3. And how much do they weigh?
4. **Eighteen** kilograms.
5. Are we going to take a taxi to the airport?
6. No, I prefer the train station. It's more comfortable.
7. Have you booked a hotel?
8. Yes, through a website. I found a hostel for **seventeen** nights.
9. And the weather forecast?
10. It says it will be humid with lightning.

✤ In Modern Greek art, numbers often symbolize national pride, with artists frequently incorporating the number 1821, the year of Greece's independence, into their works.

CHALLENGE NO. 7

ENGAGE IN A 15-MINUTE CONVERSATION
IN MODERN GREEK ON EVERYDAY TOPICS.

"Η υπομονή είναι η μητέρα της μάθησης."

"Patience is the mother of learning."

1. Θέλεις να διαβάσουμε ένα **βιβλίο** μαζί;
2. Ναι, ας διαλέξουμε ένα **μυθιστόρημα**.
3. Έχω **είκοσι ένα** βιβλία **ποίησης** και **είκοσι δύο** βιβλία **μυθοπλασίας**.
4. Ας διαβάσουμε **μυθοπλασία**. Μου αρέσει περισσότερο.
5. Εντάξει, έχω ένα που έχει **είκοσι τρία** κεφάλαια.
6. Τέλεια! Θα φτιάξω κάτι να φάμε. Έχεις προτίμηση;
7. Μπορείς να κάνεις **ζυμαρικά** με **βούτυρο** και **πιπέρι**;
8. Φυσικά, και θα προσθέσω και λίγο **κοτόπουλο**.
9. Αχ, τέλεια! Θα είναι μια υπέροχη βραδιά.

✤ In Greek, numbers 21 to 29 are formed by combining the word for "and" (και) between the units and the tens, as in "είκοσι και ένα" (twenty-one), showing a compound structure.

1. Do you want to read a **book** together?
2. Yes, let's pick a **novel**.
3. I have **twenty-one poetry books and twenty-two fiction** books.
4. Let's read **fiction**. I like it more.
5. Okay, I have one that has **twenty-three** chapters.
6. Perfect! I'll make something for us to eat. Any preferences?
7. Can you make **pasta** with **butter** and **pepper**?
8. Of course, and I'll add some **chicken** too.
9. Ah, perfect! It's going to be a wonderful evening.

✤ In Greece, Pythagoras' theorem is often humorously referred to as the "Greek tragedy" among students, highlighting the challenging yet foundational role of mathematics in education.

1. Έχεις δει το **ημερολόγιο** για το **φεστιβάλ**;
2. Ναι, το **πρόγραμμα** είναι πολύ ενδιαφέρον. Θέλω να μάθω περισσότερα για την **παράδοση** και την **ιστορία**.
3. Θα πάμε στο **μουσείο**; Είναι καλή ευκαιρία να εξερευνήσουμε τον **πολιτισμό**.
4. Καλή ιδέα! Είμαι **τουρίστας** και θέλω να μάθω όσο περισσότερα μπορώ.
5. Εγώ είμαι **ντόπιος**. Μπορώ να σε βοηθήσω. Θα είναι μια **χαλαρή** μέρα.

❖ In Greek, verbs have valency, which means they require a specific number of arguments (like subjects, objects) to form a complete sentence.

1. Have you seen the **calendar** for the **festival**?
2. Yes, the **schedule** is very interesting. I want to learn more about the **tradition** and **history**.
3. Shall we go to the **museum**? It's a good opportunity to explore the **culture**.
4. Good idea! I'm a **tourist** and I want to learn as much as I can.
5. I'm a **local**. I can help you. It will be a **relaxed** day.

✤ In Greece, the "Name Day" celebration is often considered more important than one's own birthday.

1. Σήμερα θέλω να μαγειρέψω ένα νέο **πιάτο**.
2. Ωραία! Θα χρειαστούμε το **τηγάνι** και την **κατσαρόλα**.
3. Μην ξεχάσουμε το **μαχαίρι** για τα λαχανικά και το **κουτάλι** για το αλάτι.
4. Και το **πηρούνι** για να δοκιμάσουμε αν είναι έτοιμο.
5. Μετά θα βάλουμε τα φαγητά στο **ψυγείο** ή στον **καταψύκτη**;
6. Κάποια στο **ψυγείο** και κάποια στον **καταψύκτη**. Και το πρωί, θα χρησιμοποιήσουμε την **φρυγανιέρα**.
7. Τέλεια! Θα είναι μια καλή **ημέρα** για μαγειρική.

✤ In Greek, verbs related to cooking can be transitive, needing a direct object (like "κόβω το κρέας" - "I cut the meat"), or intransitive, not needing a direct object (like "βράζω" - "I boil").

DAY 73: COOKING AND KITCHEN II

1. Today I want to cook a new **dish**.
2. Great! We will need the **pan** and the **pot**.
3. Let's not forget the **knife** for the vegetables and the **spoon** for the salt.
4. And the **fork** to test if it's ready.
5. Afterwards, shall we put the food in the **fridge** or in the **freezer**?
6. Some in the **fridge** and some in the **freezer**. And in the morning, we'll use the **toaster**.
7. Perfect! It will be a good **day** for cooking.

❖ In Greece, the culinary show "MasterChef" has significantly boosted the popularity of forgotten traditional dishes, reviving them in modern kitchens.

1. Έχω **πυρετό** και **βήχα**. Τι να κάνω;
2. Ίσως έχεις **αλλεργία**. Πρέπει να πάρεις ένα **χάπι**.
3. Έχω και **πονοκέφαλο**. Μήπως να πάω στην **κλινική**;
4. Καλύτερα να πάς στο **φαρμακείο** πρώτα. Θα σου δώσουν **υγρό** ή χάπια με **συνταγή**.
5. Και αν δεν βελτιωθώ;
6. Τότε πρέπει να επισκεφθείς την **κλινική**.

❖ In Greek, verbs related to feeling or being, like "πονάω" (to hurt) or "αρρωσταίνω" (to get sick), often don't need a direct object to make sense.

1. I have **fever** and **cough**. What should I do?
2. You might have **allergies**. You need to take a **pill**.
3. I also have a **headache**. Should I go to the **clinic**?
4. It's better to go to the **pharmacy** first. They will give you a **liquid** or pills with a **prescription**.
5. And if I don't get better?
6. Then you must visit the **clinic**.

❖ In Greece, the island of Ikaria is renowned for its extraordinarily healthy and long-lived residents, often cited as a prime example of public health success due to their lifestyle and diet.

1. Σήμερα έχουμε **μάθημα** στο **σχολείο** ή στο **πανεπιστήμιο**;
2. Στο **πανεπιστήμιο**. Πρέπει να κάνουμε **εργασίες** για τον **καθηγητή**.
3. Έχεις διαβάσει το **βιβλίο** για την **εξέταση**;
4. Ναι, αλλά πρέπει να γράψω και τις σημειώσεις μου με **στυλό**.
5. Είσαι **φοιτητής** στο πρώτο έτος;
6. Ναι, και είναι λίγο δύσκολο με όλες αυτές τις **εργασίες**.
7. Μην ανησυχείς, με τον καιρό θα γίνει ευκολότερο.

❖ In Greek, to express actions we do to ourselves, we use reflexive pronouns like "μου" (to me), "σου" (to you), and "του/της" (to him/her) right before the verb.

1. Today do we have **class** at **school** or at the **university**?
2. At the **university**. We need to do **assignments** for the **professor**.
3. Have you read the **book** for the **exam**?
4. Yes, but I need to write my notes with a **pen**.
5. Are you a **student** in your first year?
6. Yes, and it's a bit difficult with all these **assignments**.
7. Don't worry, it will get easier over time.

✤ In Greece, the world's first democratic system was born, influencing modern educational philosophies on civic engagement and critical thinking.

1. Θέλω να αγοράσω αυτό το πιάτο, πόσο κοστίζει;
2. Η **τιμή** είναι 10 ευρώ. Θα πληρώσετε με **πιστωτική κάρτα** ή **μετρητά**;
3. Με **πιστωτική κάρτα**, παρακαλώ. Μπορώ να έχω και **απόδειξη**;
4. Φυσικά, θα σας δώσω την **απόδειξη** μετά την **πληρωμή**.
5. Ευχαριστώ. Να ρωτήσω, βρίσκω αυτό το πιάτο λίγο **ακριβό**.
6. Έχουμε και πιο **φθηνά** πιάτα, αλλά αυτό είναι ποιοτικότερο.
7. Καταλαβαίνω. Ευχαριστώ για την εξυπηρέτηση.
8. Πάντα στη διάθεσή σας. Καλή συνέχεια στα ψώνια σας!

✤ In Greek, to express reciprocity, especially when talking about transactions, we often use the reflexive pronoun "μεταξύ τους" (among themselves) after the verb.

DAY 76: MONEY AND SHOPPING II

1. I want to buy this dish, how much does it cost?
2. The **price** is 10 euros. Will you pay with a **credit card** or **cash**?
3. With a **credit card**, please. Can I also have a **receipt**?
4. Of course, I will give you the **receipt** after the **payment**.
5. Thank you. May I ask, I find this dish a bit **expensive**.
6. We also have cheaper dishes, but this one is of higher quality.
7. I understand. Thank you for your service.
8. Always at your disposal. Enjoy the rest of your shopping!

❖ In Modern Greek pop culture, the iconic "Euro" bar in Athens charges just one euro for any drink, symbolizing the country's resilience and creativity in navigating economic challenges.

1. Θέλετε να παραγγείλετε από το **μενού**;
2. Ναι, ως **ορεκτικό** θα ήθελα μια **σαλάτα** και ένα **τοστ**.
3. Και για **κυρίως πιάτο**;
4. Ένα **σάντουιτς** με **μαρμελάδα**.
5. Θέλετε κάτι για **επιδόρπιο**;
6. Μια μικρή **σοκολάτα** θα ήταν τέλεια.
7. Πώς θα πληρώσετε; Με **πιστωτική κάρτα** ή **μετρητά**;
8. Με **πιστωτική κάρτα**, παρακαλώ.
9. Ευχαριστούμε πολύ. Να έχετε μια όμορφη μέρα.

❖ In Greek, to express who is doing an action for someone else, we add the agent complement using the preposition "από" followed by the person, as in "Το φαγητό μαγειρεύτηκε από τον σεφ" (The food was cooked by the chef).

1. Would you like to order from the **menu**?
2. Yes, for an **appetizer** I would like a **salad** and a **toast**.
3. And for the **main course**?
4. A **sandwich** with **jam**.
5. Would you like anything for **dessert**?
6. A small **chocolate** would be perfect.
7. How will you be paying? With a **credit card** or **cash**?
8. With a **credit card**, please.
9. Thank you very much. Have a beautiful day.

✤ In Modern Greece, the annual revival of the ancient Nemean Games honors both athletic tradition and the restoration of ancient sites, blending history with contemporary celebration.

1. Έχουμε νέο **καναπέ** στο **σπίτι**.
2. Ωραία! Και το **τραπέζι** και οι **καρέκλες**;
3. Είναι δίπλα στο **παράθυρο**. Θέλεις να δεις το **κρεβάτι**;
4. Ναι, πού είναι;
5. Δίπλα στη **πόρτα**. Και έχουμε καινούργιο **ψυγείο** και **φούρνο**.
6. Τέλεια! Και η **λάμπα**;
7. Πάνω από τη **τηλεόραση**. Σου αρέσει;
8. Πολύ! Το **σπίτι** σας είναι πολύ όμορφο.

❖ In Greek, to express doing something with an instrument or tool, we often use the preposition "με" (with) followed by the accusative case.

1. We have a new **couch** in the **house**.
2. Nice! What about the **table** and **chairs**?
3. They are next to the **window**. Do you want to see the **bed**?
4. Yes, where is it?
5. Next to the **door**. And we have a new **fridge** and **oven** too.
6. Awesome! And the **lamp**?
7. Above the **television**. Do you like it?
8. A lot! Your **house** is very beautiful.

✤ In Modern Greek homes, the color blue is often used in interior design to ward off the "evil eye," a belief dating back to ancient times.

1. Έχεις δει την **πρόγνωση** του **καιρού** για αύριο;
2. Ναι, λέει ότι θα είναι **υγρή** με **κεραυνούς** και **αστραπές**.
3. Ωχ! Φοβάμαι τις **θύελλες**. Προβλέπεται και **τυφώνας**;
4. Δεν είπαν για **τυφώνα**, αλλά μνημόνευσαν έναν **ανεμοστρόβιλο**.
5. Καλύτερα να μείνουμε μέσα. Έχεις ακούσει ποτέ για **σεισμό** ή **ηφαίστειο** εδώ;
6. Όχι, ευτυχώς εδώ δεν έχουμε τέτοια φαινόμενα. Ας ελπίσουμε να περάσει γρήγορα η κακοκαιρία.

✤ In Greek, to describe how the weather affects an activity, place the adverbial phrase of manner, like "με ήλιο" (with sun), directly after the verb, for example, "Παίζουμε έξω με ήλιο" (We play outside in sunny weather).

1. Have you seen the **weather forecast** for tomorrow?
2. Yes, it says it will be **humid** with **thunder** and **lightning**.
3. Oh no! I'm scared of **storms**. Is a **hurricane** predicted too?
4. They didn't mention a **hurricane**, but they did mention a **tornado**.
5. Better to stay inside. Have you ever heard of an **earthquake** or **volcano** here?
6. No, fortunately, we don't have such phenomena here. Let's hope the bad weather passes quickly.

❖ In Modern Greece, it's believed that if you see a halo around the moon, it means rain is coming soon.

1. Θέλεις να πάμε **σινεμά** αύριο;
2. Ναι, αλλά προτιμώ **θεατρικό έργο**. Έχεις δει την πρόγνωση του καιρού; Λέει ότι θα έχει **κεραυνούς** και **αστραπές**.
3. Ίσως να είναι καλύτερα να κάνουμε κάτι μέσα. Τι λες για **χορό**; Μπορούμε να **παίξουμε** μουσική και να τραγουδήσουμε.
4. Ακούγεται ωραία! Μετά, μπορούμε να πάμε σε ένα **εστιατόριο**. Θέλω να δοκιμάσω ένα νέο **μενού** με εξαιρετικά **ορεκτικά** και **επιδόρπιο**.
5. Εξαιρετική ιδέα! Και μετά το φαγητό, μπορούμε να πάμε για ψώνια στο **εμπορικό κέντρο**. Χρειάζομαι ένα νέο **μπουφάν**.

✤ In Greek, to express the duration of an activity, place the time complement after the verb, using the accusative case.

1. Do you want to go to the **movies** tomorrow?
2. Yes, but I prefer a **theater play**. Have you seen the weather forecast? It says there will be **thunder** and **lightning**.
3. Maybe it would be better to do something indoors. How about **dancing**? We can **play** music and sing.
4. Sounds nice! Afterward, we can go to a **restaurant**. I want to try a new **menu** with excellent **appetizers** and **dessert**.
5. Great idea! And after the meal, we can go shopping at the **mall**. I need a new **jacket**.

✤ In Greece, the game of Tavli, a form of backgammon, is so beloved that it's common to see people of all ages playing it in cafes and parks throughout the country.

CHALLENGE NO. 8

SPEAK ONLY IN MODERN GREEK FOR AN HOUR.

"Πολλές γλώσσες, πολλοί κόσμοι."

"Many languages, many worlds."

1. Θέλεις να πάμε στην πόλη με **τρένο** ή με **αυτοκίνητο**;
2. Προτιμώ με **τρένο**. Είναι πιο άνετο και δεν χρειάζεται να ανησυχούμε για το πάρκινγκ.
3. Καλή ιδέα. Μετά, θέλεις να πάμε για καφέ κοντά στο **μετρό**;
4. Ναι, ας πάμε με τα πόδια. Είναι μόνο **είκοσι τρία** λεπτά μακριά.
5. Ωραία. Μην ξεχάσεις να φέρεις το **ποδήλατο** σου αύριο. Θα κάνουμε μια βόλτα στο πάρκο.
6. Σίγουρα, δεν θα το ξεχάσω. Θα φέρω και το **κρεβάτι** για τον σκύλο μου;
7. Όχι, δεν χρειάζεται. Θα περάσει όλη την ημέρα τρέχοντας με τα **πόδια** του!

✤ In Greek, to express a location related to transport, we often use adverbs of place like "εδώ" (here) or "εκεί" (there) after the verb.

1. Do you want to go to the city by **train** or by **car**?
2. I prefer by **train**. It's more comfortable and we don't have to worry about parking.
3. Good idea. Afterwards, do you want to go for coffee near the **subway**?
4. Yes, let's walk. It's only **twenty-three** minutes away.
5. Nice. Don't forget to bring your **bicycle** tomorrow. We'll take a ride in the park.
6. Sure, I won't forget. Should I also bring my dog's **bed**?
7. No, there's no need. He'll spend the whole day running on his **legs**!

✤ In Greece, the traditional donkey paths on islands have evolved into routes for modern hiking tourism, blending ancient ways with contemporary travel.

1. Θέλεις να πάμε στο **βουνό** ή στη **λίμνη** αυτό το Σαββατοκύριακο;
2. Προτιμώ τη **λίμνη**. Είναι πιο χαλαρωτικό.
3. Και πώς θα πάμε; Με **αυτοκίνητο** ή **ποδήλατο**;
4. Με **αυτοκίνητο** είναι πιο άνετο. Έχεις δει την **πρόγνωση** του καιρού;
5. Ναι, λέει ότι θα έχει ήλιο, χωρίς **κεραυνό** ή **αστραπή**.
6. Τέλεια! Θα πάρω και τον **φίλο** μου, είναι καλός φίλος και του αρέσει η φύση.
7. Πολύ καλή ιδέα! Θα έχουμε υπέροχο Σαββατοκύριακο στη **λίμνη**.

✤ In Greek, to express the cause of an action, we use the conjunction "επειδή" (because) followed by a verb in the subjunctive mood.

1. Do you want to go to the **mountain** or the **lake** this weekend?
2. I prefer the **lake**. It's more relaxing.
3. And how will we get there? By **car** or **bicycle**?
4. By **car** is more comfortable. Have you seen the **weather forecast**?
5. Yes, it says it will be sunny, without any **thunder** or **lightning**.
6. Perfect! I'll bring my **friend** along, he's a good friend and he loves nature.
7. Great idea! We'll have a wonderful weekend at the **lake**.

❖ In Greece, the Samaria Gorge National Park, a World Biosphere Reserve, is home to the rare kri-kri (Cretan goat), once believed to be a myth, showcasing the country's commitment to preserving its unique wildlife.

1. **Χθες** το **πρωί**, πήγαμε για **πεζοπορία** στο βουνό.
2. Και **σήμερα** το **απόγευμα** τι θα κάνουμε;
3. Σκέφτομαι να πάμε για **κολύμβηση** στη λίμνη.
4. Ωραία ιδέα! Και **αύριο** το **βράδυ**;
5. Ίσως να δούμε ένα **θεατρικό έργο**. Τι λες;
6. Ναι, μου αρέσει! **Τώρα** τι κάνουμε;
7. Ας προετοιμάσουμε το δείπνο. Θα χρειαστούμε το **τηγάνι** και το **μαχαίρι**.
8. Καλή ιδέα. Θα βάλω τα πιάτα στο **τραπέζι**.
9. Και μετά, χαλάρωση στον **καναπέ**!

❖ In Greek, to express purpose, we often use the conjunction "για να" followed by the verb in the subjunctive mood.

1. **Yesterday** morning, we went **hiking** in the mountains.
2. And **today** in the **afternoon**, what are we going to do?
3. I'm thinking of going **swimming** in the lake.
4. Great idea! And **tomorrow** night?
5. Maybe we could see a **play**. What do you think?
6. Yes, I like it! **Now**, what do we do?
7. Let's prepare dinner. We'll need the **pan** and the **knife**.
8. Good idea. I'll set the **table**.
9. And after, relaxation on the **couch**!

✤ In many Greek villages, the day starts with a communal coffee at the local kafenio, where news and stories are shared as the sun rises.

1. Χθες ήμουν **ανήσυχος** για το ταξίδι με **αεροπλάνο**.
2. Γιατί; Είσαι **τρομαγμένος** από τα αεροπλάνα;
3. Όχι, αλλά είχα **πυρετό** και **βήχα**. Φοβόμουν ότι δεν θα μπορούσα να ταξιδέψω.
4. Και τώρα πώς αισθάνεσαι;
5. Τώρα είμαι **χαλαρός**. Ο **πυρετός** έφυγε και πήρα ένα **χάπι** για τον **βήχα**.
6. Αυτό είναι καλό νέο! Είσαι **περιεχόμενος** που θα ταξιδέψεις;
7. Ναι, είμαι πολύ **ενθουσιασμένος**! Και **περήφανος** που δεν άφησα την ανησυχία να με νικήσει.
8. Καλό ταξίδι λοιπόν!
9. Ευχαριστώ πολύ!

✤ In Greek, to describe someone who feels a certain emotion, we use a relative clause starting with "που" (that/who), like in "Είμαι ο άνθρωπος που νιώθει χαρούμενος" (I am the person who feels happy).

DAY 84: EMOTIONS III 🌱

1. Yesterday I was **anxious** about the trip by **plane**.
2. Why? Are you **scared** of planes?
3. No, but I had a **fever** and a **cough**. I was afraid I wouldn't be able to travel.
4. And how do you feel now?
5. Now I'm **relaxed**. The **fever** is gone and I took a **pill** for the **cough**.
6. That's good news! Are you **content** to travel?
7. Yes, I'm very **excited**! And **proud** that I didn't let the worry beat me.
8. Have a good trip then!
9. Thank you very much!

❖ In Greece, the Festival of Agios Efisios in Sardinia is a heartfelt event where thousands march in historical costumes to honor a promise made over 360 years ago, blending deep emotion with vibrant tradition.

ΗΜΈΡΑ ΝΟΎΜΕΡΟ 85: ΧΡΏΜΑΤΑ ΚΑΙ ΣΧΉΜΑΤΑ

1. Τι **χρώμα** είναι το **αυτοκίνητό** σου;
2. Είναι **μπλε**.
3. Και το δικό σου;
4. Το δικό μου είναι **κόκκινο**. Ποιο **χρώμα** σου αρέσει περισσότερο;
5. Μου αρέσει πολύ το **πράσινο**. Είναι τόσο ήρεμο.
6. Συμφωνώ. Και τι **σχήμα** προτιμάς;
7. Προτιμώ τα **στρογγυλά** αντικείμενα. Εσύ;
8. Εγώ προτιμώ τα **τετράγωνα**. Είναι πιο πρακτικά.

❖ In Greek, when describing an object with both its color and shape, you use the conjunction "και" (and) to link the two characteristics, as in "Το μπλε και τετράγωνο βιβλίο" (The blue and square book).

DAY 85: COLORS AND SHAPES

1. What **color** is your **car**?
2. It's **blue**.
3. And yours?
4. Mine is **red**. Which **color** do you like more?
5. I really like **green**. It's so calming.
6. I agree. And what **shape** do you prefer?
7. I prefer **round** objects. You?
8. I prefer **square** ones. They're more practical.

❖ In Modern Greek art, the circle often symbolizes unity and harmony, reflecting the country's deep-rooted sense of community.

1. Χθες, **συνάδελφε** μου, πήγαμε στον **αυτόματο ταμειακό μηχανισμό**.
2. Α, ναι; Και πήρατε **μετρητά**;
3. Όχι, χρησιμοποίησα την **πιστωτική κάρτα**. Και εσύ;
4. Εγώ πήρα **μετρητά** το **πρωί**.
5. Καλά έκανες. Σήμερα, θα δω τον **ξάδερφό** μου.
6. Ωραία! Εγώ θα πάω στην **γειτόνισσα**.
7. Και το **Σάββατο**;
8. Το **Σάββατο**, θα πάω σε πάρτι με τον **φίλο** μου.
9. Αχ, πόσο ωραία!

❖ In Greek, to express the reason for an action in a relationship, we use adverbial clauses introduced by words like "επειδή" (because) or "γιατί" (why), connecting two parts of a sentence to explain why something happens.

1. Yesterday, **colleague** of mine, we went to the **ATM**.
2. Oh, yes? And did you get **cash**?
3. No, I used my **credit card**. What about you?
4. I got **cash** in the **morning**.
5. Good for you. Today, I'm going to see my **cousin**.
6. Nice! I'm going to the **neighbor's**.
7. And on **Saturday**?
8. On **Saturday**, I'm going to a party with my **friend**.
9. Ah, how lovely!

✤ In Modern Greek literature, the epic friendship of Alexis Zorbas and the narrator in Nikos Kazantzakis' novel "Zorba the Greek" explores the depths of human connection beyond romantic love.

1. Σήμερα θέλω να αγοράσω **ρούχα**.
2. Τι **ρούχα** θέλεις;
3. Ένα **μπουφάν** και **παπούτσια** για το πρωί.
4. Θα πάρεις και **καπέλο** ή **γυαλιά ηλίου**;
5. Ναι, και ένα **καπέλο**. Και θέλω ένα **πουκάμισο**.
6. Για **παντελόνι** ή **φούστα** έχεις σκεφτεί;
7. Ένα **παντελόνι**. Και ίσως κάποια **αξεσουάρ**.
8. **Κολιέ ή σκουλαρίκια**;
9. Μάλλον **σκουλαρίκια**.

❖ In Greek, to compare two things, like clothing items, use "πιο" before the adjective and "από" to say "than," as in "Αυτό το παντελόνι είναι πιο άνετο από εκείνο το φόρεμα" (This pair of pants is more comfortable than that dress).

1. Today I want to buy **clothes**.
2. What **clothes** do you want?
3. A **jacket** and **shoes** for the morning.
4. Will you also get a **hat** or **sunglasses**?
5. Yes, and a **hat**. And I want a **shirt**.
6. Have you thought about **pants** or a **skirt**?
7. **Pants. And maybe some accessories**.
8. **Necklace** or **earrings**?
9. Probably **earrings**.

✤ In Modern Greek weddings, it's traditional for the bride to write the names of her single friends on the sole of her shoe, believing it will help them find love.

ΗΜΈΡΑ ΝΟΎΜΕΡΟ 88: ΤΕΧΝΟΛΟΓΊΑ ΚΑΙ ΜΈΣΑ ΕΝΗΜΈΡΩΣΗΣ ΙΙ 🌱

1. Έχεις δει τις **ειδήσεις** στην **τηλεόραση** σήμερα;
2. Όχι, άκουσα κάτι στο **ραδιόφωνο** ενώ οδηγούσα. Γιατί;
3. Υπάρχει μια ενδιαφέρουσα είδηση στο αγαπημένο μας **κανάλι**. Χρησιμοποίησα το **τηλεχειριστήριο** αλλά δεν μπορούσα να το βρω.
4. Μήπως να το ψάξουμε στον **υπολογιστή** ή στο **έξυπνο κινητό**;
5. Καλή ιδέα! Μπορούμε επίσης να τσεκάρουμε τα **κοινωνικά δίκτυα** ή να στείλουμε **ηλεκτρονικό ταχυδρομείο** στο κανάλι για περισσότερες πληροφορίες.
6. Ας το κάνουμε **σε απευθείας σύνδεση** τώρα.

✤ In Greek, to express a reason or cause, we use the conjunction "επειδή" (because) before the causal clause.

1. Have you seen the **news** on **TV** today?
2. No, I heard something on the **radio** while driving. Why?
3. There's an interesting story on our favorite **channel**. I used the **remote control** but couldn't find it.
4. Maybe we should look it up on the **computer** or **smartphone**?
5. Good idea! We can also check **social networks** or send an **email** to the channel for more information.
6. Let's do it **online** right now.

✦ In Greece, the world's first digital planetarium, the Eugenides Planetarium, combined cinema with advanced technology to offer immersive astronomical shows.

1. Τι θα πιείς; **Αναψυκτικό, νερό, χυμό, μπύρα, τσάι ή καφέ;**
2. Θα προτιμήσω ένα **καφέ.** Και εσύ;
3. Εγώ θέλω ένα **τσάι.** Και τι θα φάμε; **Κρέας, λαχανικά ή φρούτα;**
4. Ας πάρουμε **λαχανικά** και **κρέας.** Μετά, για επιδόρπιο, **φρούτα.**
5. Συμφωνώ. Και μετά, θέλεις να πιούμε **γάλα** πριν κοιμηθούμε;
6. Ναι, καλή ιδέα.

✤ If you want to say you would eat something in Greek, you use "θα" before the verb, like "Θα έτρωγα" for "I would eat."

1. What will you drink? **Soda, water, juice, beer, tea**, or **coffee**?
2. I'll have a **coffee**. How about you?
3. I want a **tea**. And what shall we eat? **Meat, vegetables**, or **fruit**?
4. Let's get **vegetables** and **meat**. Then, for dessert, **fruit**.
5. I agree. And afterwards, do you want to drink **milk** before we go to sleep?
6. Yes, good idea.

✤ In Greece, the beloved street food souvlaki is often enjoyed after a night out, symbolizing a communal end to the evening's festivities.

1. Έχεις **διαμέρισμα** ή **σπίτι**;
2. Έχω **διαμέρισμα** με όμορφο **μπαλκόνι**.
3. Πόσα **δωμάτια** έχει;
4. Δύο **δωμάτια**, ένα **σαλόνι**, **κουζίνα και μπάνιο**.
5. Ωραία! Έχεις και **κήπο** ή **αυλή**;
6. Όχι, αλλά το **μπαλκόνι** βλέπει σε έναν όμορφο **κήπο**.
7. Είμαι **χαρούμενος** για σένα! Πότε θα με καλέσεις;
8. Σύντομα! Θα κάνουμε **πεζοπορία** και μετά θα πιούμε **χυμό** στο **μπαλκόνι**.
9. Τέλεια! Ανυπομονώ!

✤ In Greek, to express actions happening at the same time, we use the conjunction "όταν" (when) followed by the verb in the subjunctive mood.

1. Do you have an **apartment** or a **house**?
2. I have an **apartment** with a beautiful **balcony**.
3. How many **rooms** does it have?
4. Two **rooms**, a **living room, kitchen, and bathroom**.
5. Nice! Do you also have a **garden** or **yard**?
6. No, but the **balcony** overlooks a beautiful **garden**.
7. I'm **happy** for you! When will you invite me?
8. Soon! We'll go **hiking** and then drink **juice** on the **balcony**.
9. Perfect! I can't wait!

✤ In Greece, the historic house of the poet Sappho on the island of Lesbos remains a mystery, as its exact location has yet to be discovered.

CHALLENGE NO. 9

WATCH A MOVIE IN MODERN GREEK WITHOUT ENGLISH SUBTITLES AND SUMMARIZE THE STORY.

"Κάθε μικρή νίκη μετράει."
"Every small victory counts."

ΗΜΈΡΑ 91: ΨΏΝΙΑ ΚΑΙ ΚΑΤΑΣΤΉΜΑΤΑ

1. Πάμε στο **σούπερ μάρκετ**;
2. Ναι, πρέπει να αγοράσουμε πράγματα για το **σπίτι**.
3. Πάρε ένα **καρότσι**, είναι πιο άνετο.
4. Κοίτα! Υπάρχουν **εκπτώσεις** στα διάφορα προϊόντα.
5. Πόσο είναι η **τιμή** αυτού του ραδιοφώνου;
6. Έχει **έκπτωση**. Κοίτα την **απόδειξη**.
7. Ας πάμε στον **ταμία** τώρα.
8. Μην ξεχάσεις να πάρεις την **απόδειξη**.
9. Τέλεια! Τώρα, πίσω στο **σπίτι**.

✤ In Greek, to express location, we use the preposition "σε" followed by the location, as in "στο μαγαζί" for "in the store."

1. Shall we go to the **supermarket**?
2. Yes, we need to buy things for the **house**.
3. Grab a **cart**, it's more comfortable.
4. Look! There are **discounts** on various products.
5. How much is the **price** of this radio?
6. It's on **discount**. Look at the **receipt**.
7. Let's go to the **cashier** now.
8. Don't forget to take the **receipt**.
9. Perfect! Now, back to the **house**.

✤ In modern Greece, the vibrant Monastiraki flea market in Athens continues the ancient Agora's tradition, blending the evolution of retail from open-air markets to bustling hubs of commerce and culture.

1. **Βοήθεια**! Υπάρχει **φωτιά** στο σπίτι δίπλα.
2. Καλέστε **αστυνομία** και **πυροσβεστική** τώρα!
   Είναι **έκτακτη ανάγκη**.
3. Ναι, καλώ αμέσως. Πρέπει να είμαστε **ασφαλείς**.
4. Έχετε **πρώτες βοήθειες**; Μπορεί να χρειαστούν.
5. Ναι, έχω στο αυτοκίνητο. Θα το φέρω.
6. Και το **ασθενοφόρο**; Να το καλέσουμε;
7. Αν κάποιος χρειάζεται **γιατρό**, ναι. Αλλά πρώτα
   να σβήσει η φωτιά.
8. Ελπίζω όλοι να είναι **ασφαλείς** και να μην
   υπάρχει **κίνδυνος**.
9. Ναι, ας ελπίσουμε. Και ας προσευχηθούμε να
   μην χρειαστεί **νοσοκομείο**.

✤ In Modern Greek, to express purpose in a final clause related to emergency and safety, we use "για να" (for/to) followed by the verb in the subjunctive mood.

1. **Help**! There is a **fire** in the house next door.
2. Call the **police** and **fire department** now! It's an **emergency**.
3. Yes, I'm calling right away. We must be **safe**.
4. Do you have **first aid**? It might be needed.
5. Yes, I have it in the car. I'll bring it.
6. And the **ambulance**? Should we call it?
7. If someone needs a **doctor**, yes. But first, the fire needs to be put out.
8. I hope everyone is **safe** and there is no **danger**.
9. Yes, let's hope. And let's pray that a **hospital** won't be necessary.

✤ In Greece, a dog named Kanellos became a symbol of resilience during protests, often seen in the front lines, seemingly protecting demonstrators.

1. Έχεις **διαβατήριο** και **βίζα**;
2. Ναι, και έκανα **κράτηση** για **εισιτήριο**.
3. Πόσες **αποσκευές** έχεις;
4. Μόνο μία **βαλίτσα** και ένα **σακίδιο πλάτης**.
5. Είσαι **τουρίστας**;
6. Ναι, ψάχνω για **οδηγό** και **χάρτη**.
7. Πάμε στο **αεροδρόμιο** τώρα;
8. Καλή ιδέα. Θα πάρουμε **ταξί**.
9. Μετά, θα πάμε στο **ξενοδοχείο**.

❖ In Greek, to express a concession or a contrast, we often use the conjunction "αν και" (even though) followed by a verb in the indicative mood.

DAY 93: TRAVEL AND PLACES III

1. Do you have a **passport** and **visa**?
2. Yes, and I've made a **reservation** for a **ticket**.
3. How many **bags** do you have?
4. Just one **suitcase** and a **backpack**.
5. Are you a **tourist**?
6. Yes, I'm looking for a **guide** and a **map**.
7. Shall we go to the **airport** now?
8. Good idea. We'll take a **taxi**.
9. Afterwards, we'll go to the **hotel**.

✤ The Grande Bretagne in Athens has hosted royalty, celebrities, and spies since 1874, witnessing pivotal moments in Greek history.

1. Έχεις **σκύλο** ή **γάτα**;
2. Έχω μια **γάτα** και ένα **πουλί**.
3. Εγώ έχω ένα **ψάρι**. Θέλω και ένα **άλογο**.
4. Τα **άλογα** είναι όμορφα. Έχεις δει **αγελάδα** στην πόλη;
5. Όχι, αλλά έχω δει **πρόβατα** και **κατσίκες** στο χωριό.
6. Και εγώ! Και μια **κότα** με **χοίρους**.

✤ In Greek, to add an explanatory clause about animals or pets, use "που" (which means "that" or "who") right after the noun, as in "Ο σκύλος που τρέχει είναι γρήγορος" (The dog that is running is fast).

1. Do you have a **dog** or a **cat**?
2. I have a **cat** and a **bird**.
3. I have a **fish**. I also want a **horse**.
4. **Horses are beautiful. Have you seen a cow** in the city?
5. No, but I have seen **sheep** and **goats** in the village.
6. Me too! And a **chicken** with **pigs**.

✤ In Greece, a pelican named Petros has become the official mascot of Mykonos, charming tourists since the 1950s.

1. Καλημέρα, **υπάλληλε**. Έχεις ετοιμάσει την **έκθεση** για την **συνάντηση**;
2. Καλημέρα, **αφεντικό**. Ναι, έχω ετοιμάσει την **έκθεση** και την **παρουσίαση**.
3. Πότε είναι η **προθεσμία**;
4. Η **προθεσμία** είναι σε είκοσι τρεις ώρες.
5. Ευχαριστώ. Πού θα γίνει η **συνάντηση**;
6. Στο μεγάλο **γραφείο**, δίπλα στο δωμάτιο του **συναδέλφου**.
7. Ωραία. Θα ενημερώσω τους **συναδέλφους**.

✤ In direct speech, we use quotation marks to repeat someone's exact words, as in: Ο δάσκαλος είπε, "Μάθετε τα επαγγέλματα".

1. Good morning, **employee**. Have you prepared the **report** for the **meeting**?
2. Good morning, **boss**. Yes, I have prepared the **report** and the **presentation**.
3. When is the **deadline**?
4. The **deadline** is in twenty-three hours.
5. Thank you. Where will the **meeting** take place?
6. In the large **office**, next to the **colleague's** room.
7. Nice. I will inform the **colleagues**.

❖ In ancient Greece, the philosopher Socrates never wrote anything down, yet his teachings profoundly shaped Western philosophy through his student Plato.

1. Τι κάνεις τη **Δευτέρα**;
2. Πάω στην εργασία. Και εσύ;
3. Εγώ έχω ραντεβού με έναν φίλο τη **Τρίτη**.
4. Ωραία! Τη **Πέμπτη** έχω συνάντηση με τον σύντροφό μου.
5. Και το **Σάββατο**;
6. Το **Σάββατο** θα πάμε σε ένα φεστιβάλ.
7. Εγώ θα επισκεφτώ την οικογένειά μου τη **Κυριακή**.
8. Α, καλά να περάσεις! Θα τα πούμε τον **Μάρτιο**.
9. Ναι, ας κάνουμε κράτηση για το φεστιβάλ.

✤ In indirect speech, when talking about days and months, the tense usually shifts back, so "σήμερα" (today) becomes "εκείνη την ημέρα" (that day), and "αυτόν τον μήνα" (this month) becomes "εκείνον τον μήνα" (that month).

1. What are you doing on **Monday**?
2. I'm going to work. And you?
3. I have a meeting with a friend on **Tuesday**.
4. Nice! On **Thursday**, I have a date with my partner.
5. And on **Saturday**?
6. On **Saturday**, we're going to a festival.
7. I'll be visiting my family on **Sunday**.
8. Oh, have a great time! We'll talk in **March**.
9. Yes, let's book for the festival.

✤ Modern Greeks still celebrate name days based on the ancient tradition of honoring saints on specific calendar dates.

1. Πονάει το **κεφάλι** μου.
2. Έχεις πυρετό; Ας δούμε με το **χέρι** μου.
3. Όχι, αλλά πονάει και το **πόδι** μου.
4. Ίσως να έπεσες και να χτύπησες τον **βραχίονα** ή το **πόδι**.
5. Μπορεί. Και το **μάτι** μου κοκκινίζει.
6. Να πάμε στον γιατρό; Μπορεί να είναι κάτι στο **αυτί** ή στη **μύτη**.
7. Ναι, καλύτερα. Δεν μπορώ να ανοίξω καλά το **στόμα** μου.
8. Θα κοιτάξει και τα **δάχτυλα** σου, μην έχεις χτυπήσει κάπου.

✤ In Greek, when talking about body and health using free indirect speech, you blend the person's thoughts or speech into your own narrative without using quotation marks or direct speech markers.

1. My **head** hurts.
2. Do you have a fever? Let's check with my **hand**.
3. No, but my **leg** also hurts.
4. Maybe you fell and hit your **arm** or **leg**.
5. Possibly. And my **eye** is turning red.
6. Should we go to the doctor? It could be something with your **ear** or **nose**.
7. Yes, better. I can't open my **mouth** well.
8. He will also check your **fingers**, in case you've hit them somewhere.

✤ In Crete, traditional "mantinades" poetry contests often accompany local wrestling matches, blending physical prowess with verbal wit.

1. Έχεις το **στυλό** μου;
2. Όχι, αλλά έχω ένα **μολύβι**. Θες;
3. Ναι, ευχαριστώ. Πρέπει να γράψω στο **τετράδιο** μου για την **εργασία**.
4. Στην **αίθουσα διδασκαλίας**, ο **δάσκαλος** είπε ότι η **εξέταση** θα είναι δύσκολη.
5. Αχ! Πρέπει να διαβάσω περισσότερο το **βιβλίο**.
6. Μην ανησυχείς. Θα σε βοηθήσω. Έχω όλες τις σημειώσεις στο **σακίδιο πλάτης** μου.
7. Ευχαριστώ πολύ! Είσαι καλός **μαθητής**.
8. Και εσύ. Ας δουλέψουμε μαζί.

✤ In Greek, the verb must agree with the subject in both number and person, so if the subject is "we" (εμείς), the verb must be in the first person plural form.

1. Do you have my **pen**?
2. No, but I have a **pencil**. Do you want it?
3. Yes, thank you. I need to write in my **notebook** for the **assignment**.
4. In the **classroom**, the **teacher** said that the **exam** will be difficult.
5. Oh! I need to read the **book** more.
6. Don't worry. I'll help you. I have all the notes in my **backpack**.
7. Thank you so much! You're a good **student**.
8. So are you. Let's work together.

❖ Aristotle, a towering figure in ancient Greek philosophy, was actually the personal tutor of Alexander the Great, shaping the mind of one of history's greatest conquerors.

ΗΜΈΡΑ ΝΟΎΜΕΡΟ 99: ΔΙΆΦΟΡΑ ΙΙ 🖋

1. Έχεις **κλειδί** για την **κλειδαριά** του **δώρου**;
2. Ναι, είναι για την **γιορτή**. Θα έχουμε **εορτασμό** με **μουσική** και **χορό**.
3. Ωραία! Σαν **φεστιβάλ**;
4. Ακριβώς, αλλά και με **παράδοση**. Θα πάμε **διακοπές** μετά;
5. Ίσως. Θα πρέπει να τελειώσω με τις **εργασίες** για το **πανεπιστήμιο** πρώτα.
6. Καταλαβαίνω. Έχεις **σακίδιο πλάτης** για τα **βιβλία**;
7. Ναι, και **τετράδιο, στυλό, μολύβι**. Όλα έτοιμα για **εξέταση**.
8. Καλή τύχη! Μετά την **εξέταση, διακοπές**!
9. Ευχαριστώ! Θα τα καταφέρω.

✤ In Greek, the typical sentence structure is Subject-Verb-Object, but it can vary for emphasis or style.

DAY 99: MISCELLANEOUS II

1. Do you have a **key** for the **lock** of the **gift**?
2. Yes, it's for the **celebration**. We will have a **celebration** with **music** and **dance**.
3. Nice! Like a **festival**?
4. Exactly, but also with **tradition**. Shall we go on **vacation** afterwards?
5. Maybe. I need to finish my **assignments** for the **university** first.
6. I understand. Do you have a **backpack** for the **books**?
7. Yes, and a **notebook, pen, pencil**. All set for the **exam**.
8. Good luck! After the **exam, vacation**!
9. Thank you! I'll make it.

✦ In Greece, it's considered good luck to spit on the bride at a wedding.

ΗΜΈΡΑ ΝΟΎΜΕΡΟ 100: ΣΥΓΧΑΡΗΤΉΡΙΑ ΓΙΑ ΤΟΝ ΟΛΟΚΛΉΡΩΣΗ ΤΟΥ ΕΓΧΕΙΡΙΔΊΟΥ ✐

1. **Φίλε**, συγχαρητήρια για την ολοκλήρωση του **βιβλίου**!
2. Ευχαριστώ πολύ! Θα πιούμε έναν **καφέ** για να το γιορτάσουμε;
3. Φυσικά! Θα έρθω με το **αυτοκίνητο** και θα σε πάρω.
4. Μην ξεχάσεις να φέρεις και λίγο **νερό**. Θα το χρειαστούμε μετά τον καφέ.
5. Θα το βάλω στην **καρέκλα** δίπλα στο **παράθυρο** για να μην το ξεχάσω.
6. Και μην ξεχάσεις το **τηλέφωνο** σου, για να βάλουμε λίγη **μουσική** ενώ οδηγούμε.
7. Όλα έτοιμα! Θα είναι ένας όμορφος εορτασμός.

❖ In Greek, every noun, adjective, and verb must agree in number, gender, and case.

DAY 100: CONGRATULATIONS ON COMPLETING THE MANUAL 🌱

1. **Friend**, congratulations on finishing the **book**!
2. Thank you so much! Shall we have a **coffee** to celebrate?
3. Of course! I'll come by **car** and pick you up.
4. Don't forget to bring some **water**. We'll need it after the coffee.
5. I'll put it on the **chair** next to the **window** so I don't forget.
6. And don't forget your **phone**, so we can play some **music** while we drive.
7. All set! It's going to be a beautiful celebration.

✤ In Modern Greek culture, smashing plates during celebrations is a traditional way to express joy and success.

CHALLENGE NO. 10

PREPARE AND GIVE AN ORAL PRESENTATION IN MODERN GREEK ON A TOPIC YOU ARE PASSIONATE ABOUT AND RECORD YOURSELF.

"Η γνώση μιας νέας γλώσσας ανοίγει την πόρτα σε μια νέα κουλτούρα."

"Knowing a new language opens the door to a new culture."

CONGRATULATIONS AND NEXT STEPS

CONGRATULATIONS

Congratulations on completing the 100 days of learning Modern Greek! Your determination and perseverance have led you to succeed in this linguistic adventure.

You are now immersed in Modern Greek and have acquired a solid vocabulary base, enabling you to understand and communicate in most everyday situations. This is a remarkable achievement in such a short time!

Throughout the lessons, you have developed mental mechanisms that encourage spontaneous understanding and natural conversation in Modern Greek.

Be proud of yourself. You have achieved a level of autonomy that fully opens up the doors to the language and culture of Modern Greek.

. . .

The adventure continues! To maintain and refine your skills in Modern Greek:

- Practice translating texts from English to Modern Greek.
- Listen to our audios on shuffle to strengthen and refresh your vocabulary.
- Immerse yourself in the language: watch movies and listen to podcasts in Modern Greek.
- If you're using Flashcards, continue their daily use.
- Communicate in Modern Greek, with native speakers or via AI.

Congratulations again on this achievement! And see you soon in your continuous learning journey. Αντίο!

WHAT'S NEXT?

Your success is undeniable, and to maintain your skills, continuous practice is essential.

Here are some ideas to continue progressing:

1. Review the vocabulary from this manual with our Flashcards.
2. Elevate your skills to a new level by discovering our intermediate-level manual or by exploring other NaturaLingua resources.
3. Join our online community: share, learn, and inspire others. Your journey can enlighten new learners.
4. Watch our video training and discover the secrets to mastering a language in just 100 days.
5. Fully immerse yourself in the language to reach new heights.

6. If you're ready for a new challenge, why not start a new language with our "Learn a Language in 100 Days" collection?

Learning a language is an endless adventure. Whether you deepen your knowledge of this language or embark on a new linguistic journey, the voyage never ends.

Congratulations and good luck on your continued journey!

ADDITIONAL RESOURCES

DOWNLOAD THE RESOURCES ASSOCIATED WITH THIS MANUAL AND GREATLY ENHANCE YOUR CHANCES OF SUCCESS.

Scan this QR code to access them:

SCAN ME

🖐 **https://www.natura-lingua.com/download**

• **Optimize your learning with audio:** To significantly improve your language skills, we strongly advise you to download the audio files accompanying this manual. This will enhance your listening comprehension and pronunciation.

• **Enhance your learning with flashcards:** Flashcards are excellent tools for vocabulary memorization. We highly encourage you to use them to maximize your results. Download our set of cards, specially designed for this manual.

• **Join our learning community:** If you're looking to connect with other language enthusiasts through "Natura Lingua", we invite you to join our online group. In this community, you'll have the opportunity to ask questions, find learning partners, and share your progress.

• **Explore more with other Natura Lingua manuals:** If you like this method, note that there are other similar manuals for different languages. Discover our complete collection of manuals to enrich your linguistic learning experience in a natural and progressive way.

We are here to support you in learning the target language. For optimal results, we highly recommend downloading the audio and using the flashcards. These additional resources are designed to further facilitate your journey.

Happy learning!

ABOUT THE AUTHOR

 François Trésorier is a passionate polyglot and an expert in accelerated learning. He has developed unique learning methods that have helped over 31,400 people in more than 94 countries quickly achieve their learning goals.

With more than 7 years of research, testing, and developing innovative approaches for rapid language learning, he created the Natura Lingua method. This intuitive and natural method, based on the latest findings in cognition, enables quick language results.

When he's not creating new language learning manuals or helping his community achieve language results, François is involved in humanitarian efforts in the south and east of Ukraine.

Discover how the Natura Lingua method can transform your language learning.

Visit our website www.natura-lingua.com and join our dynamic community of passionate learners.

SHARE YOUR EXPERIENCE

Help Us Revolutionize Language Learning

I hope you found this manual enriching and useful. Our goal is to democratize this innovative and natural approach to language learning, to help as many people as possible quickly and easily achieve their linguistic goals. Your support is crucial for us. If you enjoyed this manual, we would be deeply grateful if you could take a moment to leave a review on Amazon KDP. Your feedback is not only a source of encouragement for us but also helps other language learners discover this method. Thank you immensely for your contribution to our project and best wishes on your language learning journey!

BY THE SAME AUTHOR

FIND ALL OUR NATURALINGUA BOOKS ON OUR WEBSITE

SCAN ME

We regularly add new titles to our collection. Feel free to visit our website to discover the latest releases:

http://www.natura-lingua.com/

This list is not exhaustive:

- English in 100 Days
- Spanish in 100 Days
- German in 100 Days
- Italian in 100 Days
- Portuguese in 100 Days
- Dutch in 100 Days
- Arabic in 100 Days
- Russian in 100 Days
- Chinese in 100 Days
- Japanese in 100 Days
- Korean in 100 Days

- Ukrainian in 100 Days
- Turkish in 100 Days
- Swedish in 100 Days
- Norwegian in 100 Days
- Danish in 100 Days
- Polish in 100 Days
- Hebrew in 100 Days
- Greek in 100 Days
- Romanian in 100 Days
- Vietnamese in 100 Days

ESSENTIAL GLOSSARY

INDISPENSABLE WORDS AND THEIR MEANINGS

Above - Πάνω από	Actor/Actress - Ηθοποιός	Afternoon - Απόγευμα
Airplane - Αεροπλάνο	Airport - Αεροδρόμιο	Allergy - Αλλεργία
Alone - Μόνος/Μόνη	Alone - Μόνος	Ambulance - Ασθενοφόρο
And - Και	And you? - Εσείς;	Angry - Θυμωμένος/Θυμωμένη
Angry - Θυμωμένος	Animal - Ζώο	Anxious - Ανήσυχος
Apartment - Διαμέρισμα	App - Εφαρμογή	Appetizer - Καναπές
Appetizer - Ορεκτικό	Application - Εφαρμογή	April - Απρίλιος
Arm - Βραχίονας	Arm - Χέρι	Arrival - Άφιξη
Assistant - Βοήθεια	ATM - Αυτόματος Τραπεζικός Μηχανισμός (ATM)	ATM - Αυτόματος ταμειακός μηχανισμός
August - Αύγουστος	Aunt - θεία	Author - Συγγραφέας
Autumn - Φθινόπωρο	Back - Πλάτη	Backpack - Σακίδιο πλάτης
Bad - Κακός	Baked - Ψημένο στον φούρνο	Balcony - Μπαλκόνι
Band - Συγκρότημα	Bank - Τράπεζα	Banknote - Χαρτονόμισμα
Bar - Μπαρ	Basket - Καλάθι	Bathroom - Μπάνιο
Beach - Παραλία	Bed - Κρεβάτι	Beef - Μοσχάρι
Beer - Μπύρα	Behind - Πίσω	Beside - Δίπλα
Between - Ανάμεσα	Bicycle - Ποδήλατο	Big - Μεγάλος
Bike - Ποδήλατο	Bird - Πουλί	Black - Μαύρο

Blog - Ιστολόγιο	Blue - Μπλε	Boarding pass - Κάρτα επιβίβασης
Boat - Καράβι	Boat - Σκάφος	Book - Βιβλίο
Boss - Αφεντικό	Brain - Εγκέφαλος	Bread - Ψωμί
Brother - Αδελφός	Brown - Καφέ	Browser - Περιηγητής
Bus - Λεωφορείο	Butter - Βούτυρο	Buy - Αγοράζω
Cake - Κέικ	Calendar - Ημερολόγιο	Calm - Ήρεμος
Camera - Φωτογραφική μηχανή	Canyon - Φαράγγι	Car - Αυτοκίνητο
Cart - Καρότσι	Cash - Μετρητά	Cashier - Ταμίας
Casual - Χαλαρός	Cat - Γάτα	Cave - Σπηλιά
Ceiling - Οροφή	Celebration - Εορτασμός	Centimeter - Εκατοστόμετρο
Chair - Καρέκλα	Channel - Κανάλι	Cheap - Φθηνός
Checkout - Ταμείο	Cheese - Τυρί	Chef - Σεφ
Chest - Στήθος	Chicken - Κοτόπουλο	Chicken - Κότα
Children - Παιδιά	Chocolate - Σοκολάτα	Chocolate : Chocolate - Chocolate : Σοκολάτα
Cinema - Σινεμά	Classroom - Αίθουσα διδασκαλίας	Climate - Κλίμα
Clinic - Κλινική	Clock - Ρολόι	Close - Κοντά
Clothes - Ρούχα	Cloud - Σύννεφο	Coffee - Καφές
Coin - Κέρμα	Cold - Κρύος	Colleague - συνάδελφος

Computer - Υπολογιστής	Concert - Συναυλία	Conference - Διάλεξη
Confused - Μπερδεμένος	Content - Περιεχόμενο	Continent - Ήπειρος
Cough - Βήχας	Courtyard - Αυλή	Cousin - ξάδερφος
Cousin - Ξάδερφος/Ξαδέρφη	Cow - Αγελάδα	Credit card - Πιστωτική κάρτα
Culture - Πολιτισμός	Currency - Νόμισμα	Dance - Χορός
Danger - Κίνδυνος	Day - Ημέρα	Deadline - Προθεσμία
Debit card - Χρεωστική κάρτα	December - Δεκέμβριος	Delayed - Καθυστερημένος
Delighted - Ενθουσιασμένος	Dentist - Οδοντίατρος	Departure - Αναχώρηση
Desert - Έρημος	Dessert - Επιδόρπιο	Discount - Έκπτωση
Doctor - Γιατρός	Doctor - Γιατρός	Dog - Σκύλος
Door - Πόρτα	Down - Κάτω	Download - Κατεβάζω
Drawing - Σχέδιο	Drink - Ποτό	Drink - Πίνω
Drizzle - Ψιλόβροχο	Dry - Ξηρός	Ear - Αυτί
Earrings - Σκουλαρίκια	Earthquake - Σεισμός	Egg - Αυγό
Eight - Οκτώ	Eighteen - Δεκαοκτώ	Eleven - Έντεκα
Email - Ηλεκτρονικό ταχυδρομείο	Embassy - Πρεσβεία	Emergency - Έκτακτη ανάγκη
Employee - Υπάλληλος	Evening - Βράδυ	Exam - Εξέταση
Exchange rate - Ισοτιμία	Exchange rate - Συναλλαγματική ισοτιμία	Excited - Ενθουσιασμένος/Ενθουσιασμένη

Excited - Ενθουσιασμένος	Excuse me - Συγγνώμη	Expensive - Ακριβός
Eye - Μάτι	Face - Πρόσωπο	Family - Οικογένεια
Far - Μακριά	Fast - Γρήγορος	Father - Πατέρας
February - Φεβρουάριος	Festival - Φεστιβάλ	Fever - Πυρετός
Fiancé/Fiancée - Αρραβωνιαστικός/Αρραβωνιαστικιά	Fiction - Μυθοπλασία	Fifteen - Δεκαπέντε
Finger - Δάχτυλο	Fire - Φωτιά	Fire - Φωτιά
First aid - Πρώτες βοήθειες	Fish - Ψάρι	Fitting room - Δοκιμαστήριο
Five - Πέντε	Floor - Δάπεδο	Flower - Λουλούδι
Foot - Πόδι	Forecast - Πρόγνωση	Forest - Δάσος
Fork - Πηρούνι	Forty - Σαράντα	Four - Τέσσερα
Fourteen - Δεκατέσσερα	Freezer - Καταψύκτης	Friday - Παρασκευή
Fried - Τηγανητό	Friend - Φίλος/Φίλη	Friend - Φίλος
Friends - φίλοι	Fruit - Φρούτο	Fruits - Φρούτα
Full - Γεμάτος	Garage - Γκαράζ	Garden - Κήπος
Gate - Πύλη	Gift - Δώρο	Goat - Κατσίκα
Gold - Χρυσό	Good - Καλός	Good afternoon - Καλό απόγευμα
Good evening - Καλησπέρα	Good night - Καληνύχτα	Goodbye - Αντίο
Granddaughter - εγγονή	Grandparents - Παππούδες	Grandson - εγγονός

Grass - Χόρτο	Green - Πράσινο	Grey - Γκρι
Grilled - Ψητό	Grocery store - Μπακάλικο	Guide - Οδηγός
Hair - Μαλλιά	Hand - Χέρι	Happy - Ευτυχισμένος/Ευτυχισμένη
Happy - Ευχαριστημένος	Happy - Χαρούμενος	Hard - Σκληρός
Hat - Καπέλο	Have a good day - Καλή μέρα	Head - Κεφάλι
Headache - Πονοκέφαλος	Heavy - Βαρύς	Height - Ύψος
Hello - Καλημέρα	Here - Εδώ	Hi - Γεια
Hiking - Πεζοπορία	History - Ιστορία	Holiday - Διακοπές
Homework - Εργασίες	Homework - Εργασία	Horse - Άλογο
Hospital - Νοσοκομείο	Hospital - Νοσοκομείο	Hot - Ζεστός
Hotel - Ξενοδοχείο	Hour - Ώρα	House - Σπίτι
How are you? - Πώς είστε;	How much does it cost? - Πόσο κοστίζει;	How much? - Πόσο;
How old are you? - Πόσο χρονών είστε;	How? - Πώς;	Humid - Υγρός
Hurricane - Τυφώνας	Husband - Σύζυγος	I am - Είμαι
I am [age] years old - Είμαι [ηλικία] χρονών	I am a [profession] - Είμαι [επάγγελμα]	I am fine - Είμαι καλά
I am from [city/country] - Είμαι από [πόλη/χώρα]	I am going - Πάω	I buy - Αγοράζω
I can - Μπορώ	I give - Δίνω	I have - Έχω
I know - Ξέρω	I like music and sports - Μου αρέσει η μουσική και ο αθλητισμός	I live in [city/country] - Μένω στην [πόλη/χώρα]

I love you - Σ' αγαπώ	I miss you - Μου λείπεις	I need - Χρειάζομαι
I understand - Καταλαβαίνω	I watch - Κοιτάζω	I would like - Θα ήθελα
I'm joking - Αστειεύομαι	Ice cream - Παγωτό	Ice-cream : Ice Cream - Ice-cream : Παγωτό
In - Μέσα	Inch - Ίντσα	Indigenous - Ντόπιος
Injury - Τραύμα	Inn - Πανδοχείο	Inside - Μέσα
Internet - Ίντερνετ	Island - Νησί	Jacket - Μπουφάν
Jam - Μαρμελάδα	January - Ιανουάριος	Jewelry - Κοσμήματα
Job - Εργασία	Joyful - Χαρούμενος/Χαρούμενη	Juice - Χυμός
Juice : Juice - Juice : Χυμός	July - Ιούλιος	June - Ιούνιος
Jungle - Ζούγκλα	Key - Κλειδί	Kilogram - Κιλό
Kitchen - Κουζίνα	Knee - Γόνατο	Knife - Μαχαίρι
Lake - Λίμνη	Lamp - Λάμπα	Laptop - Φορητός υπολογιστής
Large - Μεγάλος	Lawyer - Δικηγόρος	Leaf - Φύλλο
Left - Αριστερά	Leg - Πόδι	Length - Μήκος
Lesson - Μάθημα	Light - Ελαφρύς	Lightning - Αστραπή
Liquid - Υγρό	Living room - Σαλόνι	Lock - Κλειδαριά
Long - Μακρύς	Look - Κοιτάζω	Loud - Θορυβώδης
Low - Χαμηλός	Luggage - Αποσκευές	Main course - Κυρίως πιάτο

Man - Άνδρας	Manager - Διευθυντής/Διευθύντρια	Map - Χάρτης
March - Μάρτιος	Market - Αγορά	May - Μάιος
Maybe - Ίσως	Meat - Κρέας	Medicine - Φάρμακο
Meeting - Συνάντηση	Menu - Μενού	Meter - Μέτρο
Midnight - Μεσάνυχτα	Milk - Γάλα	Milk : Milk - Milk : Γάλα
Minute - Λεπτό	Monday - Δευτέρα	Month - Μήνας
Morning - Πρωί	Mother - Μητέρα	Mountain - Βουνό
Mouse - Ποντίκι	Mouth - Στόμα	Movie - Ταινία
Museum - Μουσείο	Music - Μουσική	My name is... - Με λένε...
Near - Κοντά	Neck - Λαιμός	Necklace - Κολιέ
Neighbor - Γείτονας/Γειτόνισσα	Nephew - ανιψιός	Nervous - Νευρικός/Νευρική
Nervous - Νευρικός	New - Καινούργιος	News - Ειδήσεις
Nice to meet you! - Χάρηκα για τη γνωριμία!	Niece - ανιψιά	Night - Νύχτα
Nine - Εννιά	Nineteen - Δεκαεννιά	No - Όχι
Non-fiction - Μη-μυθοπλασία	Noon - Μεσημέρι	Nose - Μύτη
Notebook - Τετράδιο	Novel - Μυθιστόρημα	November - Νοέμβριος
Now - Τώρα	Ocean - Ωκεανός	October - Οκτώβριος
Office - Γραφείο	Okay - Εντάξει	Old - Παλιός

On the left - Αριστερά	On the right - Δεξιά	One - Ένα
Online - Σε απευθείας σύνδεση	Orange - Πορτοκαλί	Oven - Φούρνος
Over there - Εκεί	Painting - Ζωγραφική	Pan - Τηγάνι
Parents - Γονείς	Park - Πάρκο	Partner - σύντροφος
Party - Γιορτή	Passport - Διαβατήριο	Password - Κωδικός πρόσβασης
Pasta - Ζυμαρικά	Pastry : Pastry - Pastry : Ζαχαροπλαστική	Pen - Στυλό
Pencil - Μολύβι	Pepper - Πιπέρι	Pharmacy - Φαρμακείο
Photography - Φωτογραφία	Pie : Pie - Pie : Πίτα	Pig - Χοιρινό
Pill - Χάπι	Pink - Ροζ	Plane - Αεροπλάνο
Plant - Φυτό	Plate - Πιάτο	Play - Παίζω
Play - Θεατρικό έργο	Please - Παρακαλώ	Poetry - Ποίηση
Police - Αστυνομία	Police - Αστυνομία	Pond - Λίμνη
Pork - Χοιρινό	Port - Λιμάνι	Prescription - Συνταγή
Presentation - Παρουσίαση	President - Πρόεδρος	Price - Τιμή
Printer - Εκτυπωτής	Proud - Περήφανος/Περήφανη	Proud - Περήφανος
Radio - Ραδιόφωνο	Railway station - Σιδηροδρομικός σταθμός	Rain - Βροχή
Rainbow - Ουράνιο τόξο	Reading - Διάλεξη	Receipt - Απόδειξη
Red - Κόκκινο	Refrigerator - Ψυγείο	Refund - Επιστροφή χρημάτων

Relative - Συγγενής	Relaxed - Χαλαρός/Χαλαρή	Relaxed - Χαλαρός
Remote control - Τηλεχειριστήριο	Report - Έκθεση	Reservation - Κράτηση
Restaurant - Εστιατόριο	Rice - Ρύζι	Right - Δεξιά
River - Ποτάμι	Roasted - Ροστ	Roof - Στέγη
Room - Δωμάτιο	Round - Στρογγυλό	Sad - Λυπημένος/Λυπημένη
Safe - Ασφαλής	Salad - Σαλάτα	Sale - Εκπτωτική περίοδος
Sale - Εκπτώσεις	Sandwich - Σάντουιτς	Saturday - Σάββατο
Saucepan - Κατσαρόλα	Scared - Φοβισμένος	Scared - Τρομαγμένος
Schedule - Πρόγραμμα	School - Σχολείο	Screen - Οθόνη
Sea - Θάλασσα	Second - Δευτερόλεπτο	See you later - Τα λέμε αργότερα
Sell - Πουλάω	September - Σεπτέμβριος	Seven - Επτά
Seventeen - Δεκαεπτά	Shape - Σχήμα	Sheep - Πρόβατο
Ship - Πλοίο	Shirt - Πουκάμισο	Shoes - Παπούτσια
Shopping centre - Εμπορικό κέντρο	Shopping mall - Εμπορικό κέντρο	Shoulder - Ώμος
Singer - Τραγουδιστής/Τραγουδίστρια	Singing - Τραγούδι	Sister - Αδελφή
Six - Έξι	Sixteen - Δεκαέξι	Size - Μέγεθος
Skiing - Σκι	Skin - Δέρμα	Skirt - Φούστα
Slow - Αργός	Small - Μικρός	Smartphone - Έξυπνο κινητό

Snowboarding - Σνόουμπορντ	Snowflake - Νιφάδα χιονιού	Social media - Κοινωνικά δίκτυα
Soda - Αναψυκτικό	Soda : Soft Drink - Soda : Αναψυκτικό	Soft - Απαλός
Song - Τραγούδι	Sorry - Λυπάμαι	Soup - Σούπα
South - Πάνω	Spoon - Κουτάλι	Spring - Άνοιξη
Square - Τετράγωνο	Stairs - Σκάλα	Station - Σταθμός
Stop - Σταμάτα	Stop here - Σταματήστε εδώ	Store - Κατάστημα
Storm - Θύελλα	Straight ahead - Ευθεία	Stream - Ρυάκι
Stressed - Αγχωμένος	Student - Φοιτητής	Student - Μαθητής/Φοιτητής
Subject - Μάθημα	Subway - Μετρό	Suitcase - Βαλίτσα
Summer - Καλοκαίρι	Sunday - Κυριακή	Sunglasses - Γυαλιά ηλίου
Sunshine - Ηλιοφάνεια	Supermarket - Σούπερ μάρκετ	Swimming - Κολύμβηση
Table - Τραπέζι	Tall - Υψηλός	Taxi - Ταξί
Tea - Τσάι	Teacher - Δάσκαλος/Δασκάλα	Teacher - Δάσκαλος/Καθηγητής
Telephone - Τηλέφωνο	Television - Τηλεόραση	Ten - Δέκα
Terminal - Τερματικός	Thank you - Ευχαριστώ	thank you! - ευχαριστώ!
That way - Από εκεί	The day after tomorrow - Μεθαύριο	Theater - Θέατρο
There - Εκεί	Thirteen - Δεκατρία	Thirty - Τριάντα
Thirty-Eight - Τριάντα Οκτώ	Thirty-Five - Τριάντα Πέντε	Thirty-Four - Τριάντα Τέσσερα

Thirty-Nine - Τριάντα Εννιά	Thirty-One - Τριάντα Ένα	Thirty-Seven - Τριάντα Επτά
Thirty-Six - Τριάντα Έξι	Thirty-Three - Τριάντα Τρία	Thirty-Two - Τριάντα Δύο
This way - Από εδώ	Three - Τρία	Thrilled - Ενθουσιασμένος
Thunder - Κεραυνός	Thursday - Πέμπτη	Ticket - Εισιτήριο
Time - Χρόνος	Toast - Τοστ	Toast : Toast - Toast : Τοστ
Toaster - Φρυγανιέρα	Today - Σήμερα	Tomorrow - Αύριο
Tooth - Δόντι	Toothache - Οδονταλγία	Tornado - Ανεμοστρόβιλος
Tourist - Τουρίστας	Tradition - Παράδοση	Train - Τρένο
Tram - Τραμ	Tree - Δέντρο	Trolley - Καρότσι
Trousers - Παντελόνι	Truck - Φορτηγό	Tuesday - Τρίτη
Tuesday, - Τρίτη,	Turn - Στρίψε	Turn left - Στρίψτε αριστερά
Turn right - Στρίψτε δεξιά	Twelve - Δώδεκα	Twenty - Είκοσι
Twenty-Eight - Είκοσι Οκτώ	Twenty-Five - Είκοσι Πέντε	Twenty-Four - Είκοσι Τέσσερα
Twenty-Nine - Είκοσι Εννιά	Twenty-One - Είκοσι Ένα	Twenty-Seven - Είκοσι Επτά
Twenty-Six - Είκοσι Έξι	Twenty-Three - Είκοσι Τρία	Twenty-Two - Είκοσι Δύο
Two - Δύο	Uncle - θείος	Under - Κάτω
University - Πανεπιστήμιο	Up - Πάνω	Upset - Ενοχλημένος
Username - Όνομα χρήστη	Valley - Κοιλάδα	Vegetables - Λαχανικά

Visa - Βίζα	Volcano - Ηφαίστειο	Waiter/Waitress - Σερβιτόρος/Σερβιτόρα
Wall - Τοίχος	Warm - Ζεστός	Water - Νερό
Water : Water - Water : Νερό	Website - Ιστοσελίδα	Wednesday - Τετάρτη
Week - Εβδομάδα	Weekend - Σαββατοκύριακο	Weight - Βάρος
Wet - Μουσκεμένος	What day is it today? - Τι μέρα είναι σήμερα;	What do you do for a living? - Τι κάνεις στη ζωή σου;
What do you like? - Τι σου αρέσει;	What is your name? - Πώς σας λένε;	What time is it? - Τι ώρα είναι;
What? - Τι;	When? - Πότε;	Where are you from? - Από πού είσαι;
Where do you live? - Πού μένεις;	Where? - Πού;	Which one? - Ποιος; / Ποια;
White - Λευκό	Who? - Ποιος;	Why? - Γιατί;
Wi-Fi - Wi-Fi	Wide - Πλατύς	Width - Πλάτος
Wife - Σύζυγος	Window - Παράθυρο	Wine - Κρασί
Wine : Wine - Wine : Κρασί	Winter - Χειμώνας	Woman - Γυναίκα
Worried - Ανήσυχος/Ανήσυχη	Worried - Ανήσυχος	Year - Έτος
Yellow - Κίτρινο	Yes - Ναι	Yesterday - Χθες
You're welcome - Παρακαλώ	Youth hostel - Χόστελ	

Made in United States
North Haven, CT
12 December 2024

62216565R00173